REFLECT THE GLORY OF GOD IN PRAYER

HOW TO TRANSFORM YOUR PRAYER LIFE IN SEVEN SIMPLE STEPS

JOHN DAVID FALLAHEE

Book Cover by Kate Fallahee

Chapter Artwork by Olivia Fallahee

Edited by Mary Rebholz

Printed in the United States of America

www.ReflectTheGloryOfGodInPrayer.com
www.LearnLogos.com

Subject Heading: RELIGION \ CHRISTIAN LIVING \ PRAYER

REFLECT the Glory of God in Prayer
2nd ed.
ISBN 978-1-7337265-0-4

Dedicated to praying unceasingly
for my bride Stephanie
and our children: Kate, Olivia, & David.

May our Lord and Savior Jesus Christ reflect His
glory through your consecrated life of prayer to Him.

Dedicated to my brothers and sisters in the Lord
at Brookside Baptist Church.

You are an oasis of love and encouragement,
a light to the world,
faithfully living and proclaiming God's Word,
and ever growing in loving God and loving people.

Our family is thankful to be alongside you with
Christ our Redeemer shepherding us to glory.

Success and failure of the past is either
an idol of the present
or wisdom for the future. – John David Fallahee

Contents

> Ground Zero

Introduction

It was the spring of 2001 during my second semester of seminary that I enrolled in a class titled *Biblical Exposition of Prayer.* I was very excited about the topic, since Dr. James Rosscup, who had recently completed a book on every prayer of the Bible, was teaching the class. One of the requirements was to pray every day, for one hour, journaling as well, for 16 straight weeks. The other students in the class were eager to pray as well. We had visions of becoming great prayer warriors like the Apostle Paul, E.M. Bounds, and George Mueller.

However, by the end of the first week, many of us were tired and frustrated. One cried out it was legalistic to force us to pray. Another said it was an impossible assignment. Most of us ran out of ideas for prayer by the middle of the week. We were humiliated by our inability to pray effectively.

It was at that moment, I realized why so many of us struggle to pray consistently. It's hard work. It requires time, thoughtfulness, and teamwork to discover, learn, and listen to the needs of others. It entails compassion and love to hear and set aside time to pray for the needs of others. It involves an effort to faithfully pray and follow up to know how to continue in prayer. This can only be done with the help of the Holy Spirit.

At the end of the 16 weeks, we looked at each other and thanked the Lord for helping us finish the course. We desired to continue in the discipline of prayer after the class was over. Praying daily is difficult. That struggle gave birth to this book.

After that semester, I had an opportunity to preach on prayer and what I had been learning from studying all the prayers of the Bible. It was during the preparation of that sermon that the principles of *R.E.F.L.E.C.T. the Glory of God* were born.

You are probably thinking, who needs another prayer acronym, let alone one that is seven letters long! However, the approach of this book is not about formulas, methodologies, or extreme workout routines. Instead, it is about a journey through which you will grow more intimate with God. It is about being transformed into an intercessor for those in need of prayer. It is about engaging in an incredible spiritual adventure that can change lives and impact this world.

Are you ready to pray?

Let's pray!

Thank you, Father God, for the amazing opportunity at this moment to worship You! I bless You as the only All-Knowing and All-Seeing True Creator-God of the Universe. You know my thoughts from afar and hear my words before they ever reach my lips. I am but dust, weak, and frail. But You, O God, know me and my sin. You have washed me and made me clean through Your Son, My Lord and Savior Jesus Christ, through His once-for-all perfect sacrifice on Calvary.

I confess my sin and You forgive me, lift me up, and set me straight. Your Word is a lamp to my feet and a light to my path to help me face life's trials, tribulations, and triumphs. Help me to love You and love people.

I pray for those who will read this book in the future, that You will personally rescue them from sin and provide salvation and deliverance through faith in Your only begotten Son, Jesus Christ. I pray You will grow them to be steadfast and faithful in prayer, engaged as intercessors, interceding for the community around them.

May You come to my rescue in times of suffering and persecution and give me the courage and strength to endure hardship. Let me love and forgive my enemies as Your Son did on the cross praying, "Father, forgive them for they know not what they do!" I pray also, for the ones reading these words, for comfort and help in their suffering.

Help me, Father, to focus on Your kingdom. I long to see Your will done. I await the marriage of the Lamb and seeing Your Son's bride, the Church, arrayed in fine linen, clean and bright. I await the one-thousand-year reign of Your Son the Messiah, the Anointed One, Jesus Christ to rule and reign from Jerusalem with a rod of iron. I long to see Your chosen people Israel in the promised land You gave to Abraham, prospering and worshipping You in Spirit and Truth with a heart of flesh, rather than a heart of stone. Oh Father, while we wait for Your most wise plan to unfold, do not let us grow weary, but renew our youth like the eagle's.

For Your glory!
Amen.

REFLECT THE GLORY OF GOD IN PRAYER

> Step 1

Remember the Glories of God

Bless the LORD, O my soul;
And all that is within me,
bless His holy name!
Bless the LORD, O my soul,
And forget not all His benefits:
Who forgives all your iniquities,
Who heals all your diseases,
Who redeems your life from destruction,
Who crowns you with lovingkindness
and tender mercies,
Who satisfies your mouth with good things,
So that your youth is renewed like the eagle's.
King David (Psalm 103:1-5)

Let us enter the throne room of God and see prayer from another perspective. Travel with me to a future time and let us reverently look into the Holy Place.

> When He opened the seventh seal, there was silence in heaven for about half an hour. And I saw the seven angels who stand before God, and to them were given seven trumpets. Then another angel, having a golden censer, came and stood at the altar. He was given much incense, that he should offer it with the prayers of all the saints upon the golden altar which was before the throne. And the smoke of the incense, with the prayers of the saints, ascended before God from the angel's hand. (Revelation 8:1-4)

This vision of the future was written down by John, one of the 12 apostles of Jesus Christ. On earth, terrible judgments are being released upon mankind for their sin and rebellion. Jesus describes this time as the "Great Tribulation." People are panicking and perishing, but amidst this chaos and persecution, believers are praying. They are remembering their God.

Revelation 8:1-4 provides a glimpse into the throne room of God, which is filled with the smoke of incense and the prayers of the saints. Amazing! This makes me wonder if there are days where there is less smoke of the incense, because believers are praying less. I wonder if the angels sorrow at such prayerlessness. It certainly grieves God when His people do not seek His face nor remember Him daily.

Did you know there was an earthly counterpart to this heavenly scene? In Israel, the Jewish people had an incense offering. In Luke 1:8-11, we find Zechariah (John the Baptist's father) performing the ritual.

> So it was, that while he was serving as priest before God in the order of his division, according to the custom of the priesthood, his lot fell to burn incense when he went into the temple of the Lord. And the whole multitude of the people was praying outside at the hour of incense. Then an angel of the Lord appeared to him, standing on the right side of the altar of incense. (Luke 1:8-11)

This offering is reminiscent of Psalm 141:2 "Let my prayer be set forth before thee as incense..." Prayer begins with acknowledging God. This is the first crucial step in praying more effectively.

△ STEP 1 △
REMEMBER THE GLORIES OF GOD

Let me ask you a several questions:

- Do you know who God is? What He loves? What He hates? What He has done in the past? What He will do in the future? Can you recall from the Scriptures His attributes, His names, and His commandments?

- Are your prayers limited by a lack of knowledge about God? How do you praise God? Do you thank God, and if so, for what?

- Have you considered that the heights of intimate worship through prayer are linked to a deep understanding of God and His Word? Later, we will consider the prayers of Moses, David, Solomon, Daniel, and Paul who knew God and His Word intimately.

Question: So how does one remember the glories of God in prayer? How should our prayers begin?

I am convinced that as you study the Bible to know God more deeply, your prayer life will be transformed. Do you want to grow closer to God? Then begin by asking God to give you a greater passion for prayer and curiosity to know and think rightly about Him.

To help you in your journey to pray more effectively, let me introduce five individuals who wanted to grow closer to God. May these examples kindle afresh in you a deeper passion for remembering the glories of God in your prayers.

Moses

Moses knew God, worshipped God, and desired to know God more intimately.

> And he said, "Please, show me Your glory."
> (Exodus 33:18)

What an astonishing request. Moses was passionate about God and His glory. This is an excellent beginning to prayer. So, what did Moses see after He prayed?

> And the LORD passed before him and proclaimed, "The LORD, the LORD God, merciful and gracious, longsuffering, and abounding in goodness and truth, keeping mercy for thousands, forgiving iniquity and transgression and sin, by no means clearing the guilty, visiting the iniquity of the fathers upon the children and the children's children to the third and the fourth generation." So Moses made haste and bowed his head toward the earth, and worshiped.
> (Exodus 34:6–8)

What an amazing revelation. Moses receives additional insight about God. He understands that God pardons as well as punishes sin. Moses bows low and worships in reverence.

Now keep in mind, what Moses saw and heard was incredible, and that was over 3500 years ago. A lot has taken place since then. We have the glory of God revealed through Jesus Christ. We now stand on the other side of His cross. We have more revelation that reveals the glory of God in more detail. This desire to see the glory of God is important, but it must not be for self only.

Question: Do you desire others to see and know the glory of God? Do you pray for others to know God's glory and the glory of His Son?

Paul the Apostle

Paul was an incredible theologian and evangelist. He loved God and he loved people. He desired and prayed that others would seek after the glory of God.

> The eyes of your understanding being enlightened; that you may know what is the hope of His calling, what are the riches of the glory of His inheritance in the saints (Ephesians 1:18)

Paul was always praying for others to see God's glory. When we pray, we must be thinking of others and not just ourselves. When you think of someone who does not know Christ, nor understands the free grace gift of forgiveness by faith alone, do you pray that they would see the glory of God? Would you dare to pray that God the Father would send to them faithful Christians to share the Gospel? Are you praying that God would help your witness to better reflect Christ's manner of grace and truth? Would you pray that they would be open to reading the Bible?

Question: How do you keep your vision of God fresh and accurate? How do know that you are thinking correctly and accurately about God and His glory?

Solomon

Solomon, when he was younger, meditated often on the glory of God's character. When Solomon had completed building the temple for the Lord, his prayer was filled with references to the person, character and glory of God. His entire prayer is found in 2 Chronicles 6:12–42. Here are three portions from that prayer. As you are reading, notice Solomon's reflection on the glory of God.

> and he said: "LORD God of Israel, *there is* no God in heaven or on earth like You, who keep *Your* covenant and mercy with Your servants who walk before You with all their hearts." (2 Chronicles 6:14)

> But will God indeed dwell with men on the earth? Behold, heaven and the heaven of heavens cannot contain You. How much less this temple which I have built! (2 Chronicles 6:18)

> "O LORD God, do not turn away the face of Your Anointed; Remember the mercies of Your servant David." When Solomon had finished praying, fire came down from heaven and consumed the burnt offering and the sacrifices; and the glory of the LORD filled the temple. And the priests could not enter the house of the LORD, because the glory of the LORD had filled the LORD's house. When all the children of Israel saw how the fire came down, and the glory of the LORD on the temple, they bowed their faces to the ground on the pavement, and worshiped and praised the LORD, saying: "For He is good, For His mercy endures forever."
> (2 Chronicles 6:42–7:3)

Now your prayers probably won't result in fire coming down from heaven nor be followed by the glory of God filling the church, but do you see how Solomon's prayer reflects the glory of God? This kind of prayer is the overflow of much meditation on the glory of God.

Question: Are you able to describe the glory of God to others? Do you know your Bible well enough to explain the glory of God?

Jonathan Edwards

Jonathan Edwards was a pastor during the revivals at Northampton in 1734 and 1735. The following excerpt is from his sermon *Ruth's Resolution* preached in April 1735.

> "...God is a glorious God. There is none like Him, Who is infinite in glory and excellency. He is the most high God, glorious in holiness, fearful in praises, doing wonders. His name is excellent in all the earth, and His glory is above the heavens. Among the gods there is none like unto Him; there is none in heaven to be compared to Him, nor are there any among the sons of the mighty that can be likened unto Him God is the fountain of all good and an inexhaustible fountain; He is an all-sufficient God, able to protect and defend and do all things for them: he is the King of glory, the Lord strong and mighty, the Lord mighty in battle: a strong rock, and a high tower. There is none like the God of Jeshurun, Who rideth on the heaven and in His excellency on the sky. The eternal God is a refuge, and underneath are everlasting arms. He is a God who hath all things in his hands, and does whatsoever He pleases. He killeth and maketh alive; He bringeth down to the grave and bringeth up; He maketh poor and maketh rich. The pillars of the earth are the Lord's. God is an infinitely holy God. There is none holy as the Lord. And He is infinitely good and merciful. Many that others worship and serve

> as gods, are cruel beings, spirits that seek the ruin of souls; but this is a God that delighteth in mercy; His grace is infinite, and endures forever. He is love itself, an infinite fountain and ocean of it."

Wow! Where does such an understanding of God's glory come from? The Scriptures. Edwards' knowledge of God's glory is a byproduct of much prayer, study, and meditation on the Scriptures. This is a man who has spent a lot time studying the character and works of God.

Question: How often do you meditate on the glory of God? Do you frequently think about His magnificent works and transcendent written Word?

The Psalmist

Have you ever visited NASA's website where they reveal the pictures and videos of various space probes? Once, I was reading about the space probe, Cassini, which studied the planet Saturn. Its mission began in October 1997 and ended by purposely crashing into the planet in September 2017. You can learn more by visiting the website and reviewing the images at https://solarsystem.nasa.gov/missions/cassini. When the mission was completed, the scientists high-fived one another for their mission's accomplishments. But how many of us acknowledge the effortless work of the Creator who made everything in the universe?

The psalmist by inspiration of the Holy Spirit, having never seen Saturn, describes the heavens with a beautiful poem from his vantage point on earth.

> The heavens declare the glory of God; And the firmament shows His handiwork. Day unto day utters speech, And night unto night reveals knowledge. *There is* no speech nor language *Where* their voice is not heard. Their line has gone out through all the earth, And their words to the end of the world. In them He has set a tabernacle for the sun, Which *is* like a bridegroom coming out of his chamber, *And* rejoices like a strong man to run its race. Its rising *is* from one end of heaven, And its circuit to the other end; And there is nothing hidden from its heat. (Psalm 19:1–6)

The psalmist does not end here. He moves from describing God's general revelation, His creation, to describing God's special revelation, His Scriptures.

> The law of the LORD *is* perfect, converting the soul; The testimony of the LORD *is* sure, making wise the simple; The statutes of the LORD *are* right, rejoicing the heart; The commandment of the LORD *is* pure, enlightening the eyes; The fear of the LORD *is* clean, enduring forever; The judgments of the LORD *are* true *and* righteous altogether. More to be desired *are they* than gold, Yea, than much fine gold; Sweeter also than

> honey and the honeycomb. Moreover by them Your servant is warned, *And* in keeping them *there is* great reward. Who can understand *his* errors? Cleanse me from secret *faults*. Keep back Your servant also from presumptuous *sins;* Let them not have dominion over me. Then I shall be blameless, And I shall be innocent of great transgression. Let the words of my mouth and the meditation of my heart Be acceptable in Your sight, O LORD, my strength and my Redeemer. (Psalm 19:7–14)

Now toward the end of the Psalm, he worships God, confesses his sin, asks for forgiveness, and desires to walk in holiness. Remembering the glories of God transforms you from the inside out. We need such a renewal of our inner spiritual life.

Remembering the glories of God is not just about keeping a list of truths, or even recalling vital facts. It is necessary to avoid thinking incorrectly about God. I am sure you have experienced the upsetting moment when others thought wrongly about you. How much more serious it is to think wrongly about the character, nature, and person of God. If people are willing to sue for great sums of money over slander of character, may we be ever so careful to think rightly about God.

Remembering the glories of God is one of the best ways to begin prayer. It honors Him as the preeminent One and helps center your prayer on Him rather than centering the prayer on you. You may need to dig deeper in Bible study so that you have something to say to God. But this is a worthwhile endeavor that will grow you in the knowledge of our great God. I can think of no better way to begin praying than by praising and adoring our amazing God and Savior, remembering the wonderful things He has done.

PRAYER EXAMPLE

Lord, you are merciful and gracious, slow to anger, and abounding in mercy. (Psalm 103:8)

Great are You Father God. You are to be praised greatly! Your greatness is unsearchable. (Psalm 145:3)

I praise You for rescuing Noah and his family in the ark from the flood judgment and for the way You rescue sinners from eternal judgment through Jesus Christ our Ark of salvation. (1 Peter 3:18–22)

YOUR PRAYER

CHAPTER SUMMARY

Step 1 – Remember the Glories of God

- **Moses:** Desire to see the glory of God (Exodus 33:18)
- **Paul:** Desire others to see the glory of God (Ephesians 1:18)
- **Solomon:** Meditate often on the glory of God (2 Chronicles 6:13–7:3)
- **Jonathan Edwards:** Proclaim the glory of God to others (*Ruth's Resolution,* Ruth 1:16)
- **The Psalmist:** Confess your sin and walk in holiness as a response to His creation and His written Word (Psalm 19)

GROUP DISCUSSION

1. Share with each other a truth or an event about God's glory from the Scriptures. You may wish to write these down and pray through them to God.

2. Describe an attribute of God that comforts you in times of difficult circumstances.

3. Pick one passage to memorize and apply this week that reflects a truth about God's glory. Be sure to share your experience with someone.

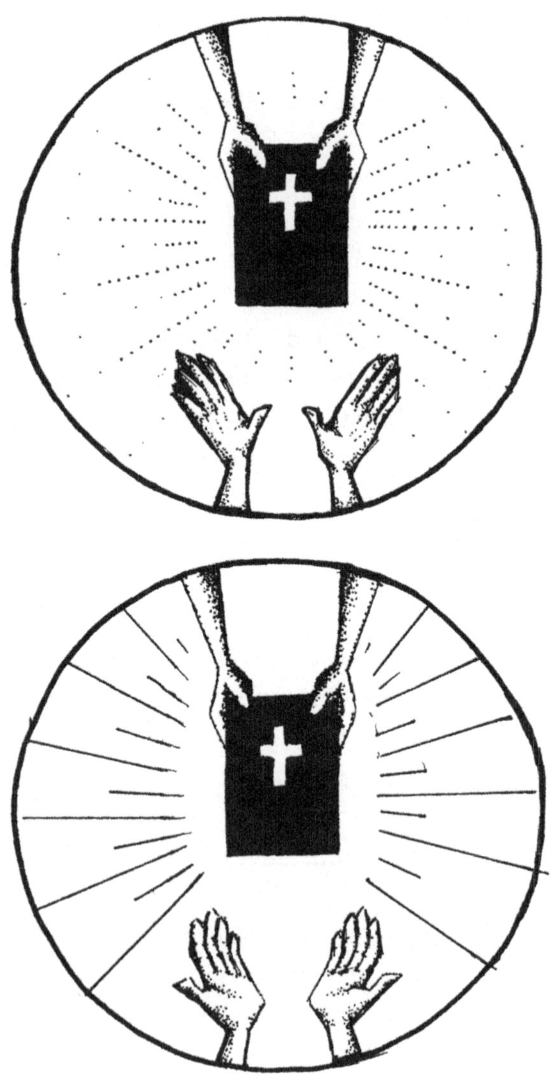

> Step 2

Examine your Motives & Manner

"And when you pray,
you shall not be like the hypocrites.
For they love to pray standing in the synagogue
and on the corners of the streets,
that they may be seen by men.
Assuredly, I say to you, they have their reward.
But you, when you pray, go into your room,
and when you have shut your door,
pray to your Father who is in the secret place;
and your Father who sees in secret will reward you
openly. And when you pray,
do not use vain repetitions as the heathen do.
For they think that they will be heard
for their many words.
Jesus Christ (Gospel of Matthew 6:5-7)

After focusing on the person and work of God, we now travel from the throne room of God to the innermost part of our being, our heart and mind. When it comes to praying to God, remembering He knows all and sees all is both a comfort and a warning.

Ways & Words

The passage at the beginning of the chapter is an important reminder that God hates the ways of pride and hypocrisy. Interestingly, He also dislikes prayers that repeat the same words over and over. God wants an honest conversation in prayer, not "vain repetition." These are solemn reminders regarding our mindset before we enter the prayer closet. What is the right kind of spirit for prayer? Psalm 34:18 affirms that the Lord appreciates a broken heart and contrite spirit in prayer.

Question: When you pray, are you captivated by God or something else? How do you keep yourself focused on God in prayer?

When my children were around the ages of 6, 4 and 2, I would find them clutching their favorite stuffed animal when we were praying to God. As lovingly as possible, I would remind them to give their full attention to the Lord and to put away their toys. As adults we too must guard our mind and heart against clutching anything that would distract us in prayer.

Therefore, we must examine our motives and manner in prayer.

△ STEP 2 △
EXAMINE YOUR MOTIVES & MANNER

Take a moment to reflect on the last four prayers you prayed. Then on the lines below list whether the prayer was about you, another believer, an unbeliever, or God. If you have not prayed recently and cannot recall the content of your prayers, simply note the approximate date when you last prayed.

1.____

2.____

3.____

4.____

What did you discover about yourself and the focus of your prayers? Were your prayers evenly balanced? Were more prayers for you than for others? If you are feeling discouraged at the moment, then please put this book down and pray right now. Admit and confess to God the areas where you are falling short and praise Him for the areas that are going well. Ask Him right now to help you excel still more in prayer.

Question: How do we guard our attitudes and actions in prayer? How do I know if my prayers are acceptable and pleasing to God?

Let me share with you several critical areas to consider before you worship God in prayer. Let's ready ourselves to approach God with reverence, respect, and holy devotion. He is worthy of our worship.

Prayerlessness & Lust

The Book of James was written by the half-brother of Jesus. After Jesus was born, Mary and Joseph had other children. James would later become a central figure and leader in the early church. In the book that bears his name, he discusses prayer.

> Where do wars and fights *come* from among you? Do *they* not *come* from your *desires for* pleasure that war in your members? You lust and do not have. You murder and covet and cannot obtain. You fight and war. Yet you do not have because you do not ask. You ask and do not receive, because you ask amiss, that you may spend *it* on your pleasures. Adulterers and adulteresses! Do you not know that friendship with the world is enmity with God? Whoever therefore wants to be a friend of the world makes himself an enemy of God. (James 4:1–4)

James reveals by inspiration of the Holy Spirit that the manner and behavior of some Christians had become spiritually compromised in the church. They were worldly. You could no longer tell the difference between a Christian and non-Christian by their words and deeds. They no longer loved one another. They were fighting, coveting, and lusting. God grieves when His children sin.

As a result, some became prayerless. Discontentment and impatience impeded their prayers. Others in the church were praying; but their motives in prayer were selfish, materialistic, and earthly.

Over the years I have counseled individuals and couples in sin. The root problem was the same in every case. Troubles began when they stopped praying. If you are married and are not praying together, go right now to your spouse, seek the Lord immediately, confess to Him your failure to pray as a couple, and repent by praying daily together. I strongly urge you to memorize James 4:1-4 as a protection against prayerlessness, asking amiss, and worldliness.

Question: Did you know your prayers may not be heard by God due to your unloving behavior? What if God refused to listen to your prayers?

Impenetrable Ceilings

Our relationship with God and others plays a significant role in whether our prayers will be heard or hindered. Consider the following passage directed toward husbands who fail to honor their wives.

> Husbands, likewise, dwell with *them* with understanding, giving honor to the wife, as to the weaker vessel, and as *being* heirs together of the grace of life, that your prayers may not be hindered. (1 Peter 3:7)

I remember the first time I read this as a single person, I thought to myself, "I better love my future wife. Otherwise, my prayers will never make it past the ceiling!"

How can someone who claims to love God, dishonor their wife, and expect answered prayer? God is opposed to such hypocrisy. Never forget that the manner in which you are living is directly connected to the effectiveness of your prayers. James would later write in James 5:16 "...The effective, fervent prayer of a righteous man avails much."

Question: Are you living a holy life right now? Could others tell by your actions alone that you are building upon Christ the Rock and His Word?

Quiet & Peaceable life

We live in tumultuous times. It seems every week there is some conflict, crisis, or catastrophe. There is much to pray about these days. It was not that much different for the early church. What is Paul's advice?

> Therefore I exhort first of all that supplications, prayers, intercessions, *and* giving of thanks be

> made for all men, for kings and all who are in authority, that we may lead a quiet and peaceable life in all godliness and reverence. For this *is* good and acceptable in the sight of God our Savior, who desires all men to be saved and to come to the knowledge of the truth. For *there is* one God and one Mediator between God and men, *the* Man Christ Jesus, who gave Himself a ransom for all, to be testified in due time, for which I was appointed a preacher and an apostle—I am speaking the truth in Christ *and* not lying—a teacher of the Gentiles in faith and truth.
> (1 Timothy 2:1–7)

What an important reminder for today. May this be the consistent pattern of our life before God, authority, and others. You might be thinking, "John, how in the world is this done?"

First, be sure to look at Appendix 4. There you will find a list of twelve prayer categories. This will help focus your prayers on essential topics. Second, examine Appendix 5 for creating a simple prayer journal. Third, remember that prayer begins by asking, persevering, and watching for answered prayer. Below are three key passages on these three ideas.

Asking

> "Ask, and it will be given to you; seek, and you will find; knock, and it will be opened to you. For

everyone who asks receives, and he who seeks finds, and to him who knocks it will be opened. Or what man is there among you who, if his son asks for bread, will give him a stone? Or if he asks for a fish, will he give him a serpent? If you then, being evil, know how to give good gifts to your children, how much more will your Father who is in heaven give good things to those who ask Him!" (Matthew 7:7–11)

Persevering

Then He spoke a parable to them, that men always ought to pray and not lose heart, saying: "There was in a certain city a judge who did not fear God nor regard man. Now there was a widow in that city; and she came to him, saying, 'Get justice for me from my adversary.' And he would not for a while; but afterward he said within himself, 'Though I do not fear God nor regard man, yet because this widow troubles me I will avenge her, lest by her continual coming she weary me.' " Then the Lord said, "Hear what the unjust judge said. And shall God not avenge His own elect who cry out day and night to Him, though He bears long with them? I tell you that He will avenge them speedily. Nevertheless, when the Son of Man comes, will He really find faith on the earth?" (Luke 18:1–8)

Watching

> "But take heed to yourselves, lest your hearts be weighed down with carousing, drunkenness, and cares of this life, and that Day come on you unexpectedly. For it will come as a snare on all those who dwell on the face of the whole earth. Watch therefore, and pray always that you may be counted worthy to escape all these things that will come to pass, and to stand before the Son of Man." (Luke 21:34–36)

In the early days of my walk with the Lord, I started a new job and prayed for an opportunity to witness at work. Shortly thereafter, an individual would visit my cubicle often, interrupting my work. I was becoming concerned that my new boss would see me talking rather than working. In mentioning this in passing to my wife, she reminded me about my earlier prayer. Ugh! I asked, but I did not persevere in prayer or remain watching. If you struggle with asking, persevering, or watching, try keeping a prayer journal and review it often.

PRAYER EXAMPLE

My sin is always before me. Against You, You only, have I sinned and done this evil in Your sight. (Psalm 51:3-4)

I confess the following sins to you Father... (1 John 1:9)

Wash me thoroughly from my sin and cleanse me. (Psalm 51:2)

YOUR PRAYER

CHAPTER SUMMARY

Step 2 – Examine Your Motives & Manner

- **Ways & Words** (Matthew 6:5-7)
- **Prayerlessness & Lust** (James 4:1-4)
- **Impenetrable Ceilings** (1 Peter 3:7)
- **Quiet & Peaceable life** (1 Timothy 2:1–7)
- **Asking** (Matthew 7:7-11)
- **Persevering** (Luke 18:1-8)
- **Watching** (Luke 21:34-36)

GROUP DISCUSSION

1. What are some of the obstacles you have faced in the past that derailed your prayer life?

2. Have you experienced seasons of prayerlessness? Why or why not? Are you struggling with prayerlessness and need help to return to praying regularly?

3. Are you leading a quiet and peaceable life?

4. Compile a list of those in authority at the local, state, and federal level and begin praying for those in authority.

> Step 3

Face Life with the Scriptures

When He came to the place, He said to them,
"Pray that you may not enter into temptation."
And He was withdrawn from them about a stone's
throw, and He knelt down and prayed, saying,
"Father, if it is Your will, take this cup away from Me;
nevertheless not My will, but Yours, be done."
Then an angel appeared to Him from heaven,
strengthening Him. And being in agony,
He prayed more earnestly.
Then His sweat became like great drops of blood
falling down to the ground.
When He rose up from prayer,
and had come to His disciples,
He found them sleeping from sorrow.
Then He said to them, "Why do you sleep?
Rise and pray, lest you enter into temptation."
Jesus Christ (Gospel of Luke 22:40-46)

After many months of reading the Bible, praying to God, seeking Jesus Christ for deliverance from my sin, confessing my sin, and struggling with the truths of the Scriptures, God in His mercy granted me repentance and faith (2 Timothy 2:25), and I repented and believed (Romans 10:9–13). By His grace through faith, God gifted me salvation (Ephesians 2:8-9), forgave all my sin, adopted me as His child, and delivered me from my addictions (Romans 8:12–17). God placed the Holy Spirit in me. I was born again (John 3:1–21) and made new (2 Corinthians 5:17). Praise be to God!

This principle of facing life with the Scriptures is not a "one and done." Rather it is a daily pattern and practice of true believers.

△ STEP 3 △
FACE LIFE WITH THE SCRIPTURES

Question: What do the following individuals have in common?

- A childless wife in a polygamous marriage
- A teenager taken captive by enemies
- A 26-year-old king reforming a nation

Answer: These three individuals were in difficult circumstances, sought God in prayer, and faced life with the Scriptures.

Hannah

It was the time of the judges and there was no king. Everyone did what was right in their own eyes. There were wars and famines. It was a troublesome time.

When the Bible introduces us to Hannah, she is at the lowest point in her life. She is driven to despair by her circumstances and this drives her to the Lord in prayer.

> And whenever the time came for Elkanah to make an offering, he would give portions to Peninnah his wife and to all her sons and daughters. But to Hannah he would give a double portion, for he loved Hannah, although the LORD had closed her womb. And her rival also provoked her severely, to make her miserable, because the LORD had closed her womb. So it was, year by year, when she went up to the house of the LORD, that she provoked her; therefore she wept and did not eat. Then Elkanah her husband said to her, "Hannah, why do you weep? Why do you not eat? And why is your heart grieved? *Am* I not better to you than ten sons?" So Hannah arose after they had finished eating and drinking in Shiloh. Now Eli the priest was sitting on the seat by the doorpost of the tabernacle of the LORD. (1 Samuel 1:4-9)

Life has a way of squeezing out what is truly inside. Let's see what flows out from Hannah's heart.

> And she *was* in bitterness of soul, and prayed to the LORD and wept in anguish. Then she made a vow and said, "O LORD of hosts, if You will indeed look on the affliction of Your maidservant and remember me, and not forget Your maidservant, but will give Your maidservant a male child, then I will give him to the LORD all the days of his life, and no razor shall come upon his head. (1 Samuel 1:10–11)

Do you see the intense emotion inside of her? Can you relate to the bitterness of her soul? That bitterness unleashes a flood of tears and she weeps in anguish. Yet, in spite of this pain, Hannah vows to give her first child over to the Lord to serve Him. Hannah faces life with tears and truth. Amazingly, the Lord answers her prayer and Samuel the judge, prophet, and kingmaker is born.

Question: How was she able to walk this way in faith? How was she able to make such a sacrifice?

It is not until the next chapter that we discover the depths of her knowledge of the Scriptures and God.

> And Hannah prayed and said: "My heart rejoices in the LORD; My horn is exalted in the LORD. I smile at my enemies, Because I rejoice in Your salvation. "No one is holy like the LORD, For *there is* none besides You, Nor *is there* any rock like our God. "Talk no more so very proudly; Let no

arrogance come from your mouth, For the LORD *is* the God of knowledge; And by Him actions are weighed. "The bows of the mighty men *are* broken, And those who stumbled are girded with strength. *Those who were* full have hired themselves out for bread, And the hungry have ceased *to hunger.* Even the barren has borne seven, And she who has many children has become feeble. "The LORD kills and makes alive; He brings down to the grave and brings up. The LORD makes poor and makes rich; He brings low and lifts up. He raises the poor from the dust *And* lifts the beggar from the ash heap, To set *them* among princes And make them inherit the throne of glory. "For the pillars of the earth *are* the LORD's, And He has set the world upon them. He will guard the feet of His saints, But the wicked shall be silent in darkness. "For by strength no man shall prevail. The adversaries of the LORD shall be broken in pieces; From heaven He will thunder against them. The LORD will judge the ends of the earth. "He will give strength to His king, And exalt the horn of His anointed."
(1 Samuel 2:1–10)

This is an amazing prayer. It speaks of the Lord's salvation, His humbling of the proud, His love for his people, His future judgment, and the Messiah's future rule and reign. Hannah had to be saturated with these truths beforehand in order to pray through these great themes of the Scriptures. May you find encouragement and hope in Hannah's example as she faced life with the Scriptures, both in the 'desert valleys' and 'mountain peaks' of life.

Daniel

It was 605 B.C., and Jerusalem was besieged by King Nebuchadnezzar. Daniel was one of the captives hauled off to the nation of Babylon where he was forced to serve in the king's court. Daniel loved and obeyed the Lord.

While Daniel was serving, King Nebuchadnezzar has a dream and demands that the leadership of his court guess and interpret the dream. Since no man has such abilities, everyone in the court refused to guess knowing they would be killed if they were incorrect. So out of frustration and anger, King Nebuchadnezzar decrees that all his wise men should be slain.

> Then with counsel and wisdom Daniel answered Arioch, the captain of the king's guard, who had gone out to kill the wise *men* of Babylon; he answered and said to Arioch the king's captain, "Why is the decree from the king so urgent?" Then Arioch made the decision known to Daniel. So Daniel went in and asked the king to give him time, that he might tell the king the interpretation. Then Daniel went to his house, and made the decision known to Hananiah, Mishael, and Azariah, his companions, that they

might seek mercies from the God of heaven concerning this secret, so that Daniel and his companions might not perish with the rest of the wise *men* of Babylon. Then the secret was revealed to Daniel in a night vision. So Daniel blessed the God of heaven. Daniel answered and said: "Blessed be the name of God forever and ever, For wisdom and might are His. And He changes the times and the seasons; He removes kings and raises up kings; He gives wisdom to the wise And knowledge to those who have understanding. He reveals deep and secret things; He knows what *is* in the darkness, And light dwells with Him. "I thank You and praise You, O God of my fathers; You have given me wisdom and might, And have now made known to me what we asked of You, For You have made known to us the king's demand. (Daniel 2:14–23)

Question: Did you notice how Daniel used wisdom with the captain of the guard? Did you notice how he sought help from his friends in prayer?

God answered Daniel's request, and Daniel blesses God. What an excellent model of prayer, facing life with the Scriptures. I love the end of this passage, it is so rich with truths regarding the sovereignty of God and His omniscience, knowing all things. Daniel knew God, studied His Word, and as a result was able to face life with the Scriptures.

Josiah

Imagine if there were no Bibles? That was the state of affairs during the reign of Josiah in Judah. He became king when he was only eight years old. The kingdom was idolatrous and rebellious. One day, when the king was about 26 years old, the high priest discovered a copy of the Law (2 Kings 22:8). Upon hearing the Scriptures read, King Josiah tore his clothes in great grief over the sin of the people against God and His Word (2 Kings 22:11). Josiah sent the priest, scribe, and several others to inquire of the Lord.

> Then the king commanded Hilkiah the priest, Ahikam the son of Shaphan, Achbor the son of Michaiah, Shaphan the scribe, and Asaiah a servant of the king, saying, "Go, inquire of the LORD for me, for the people and for all Judah, concerning the words of this book that has been found; for great *is* the wrath of the LORD that is aroused against us, because our fathers have not obeyed the words of this book, to do according to all that is written concerning us." So Hilkiah the priest, Ahikam, Achbor, Shaphan, and Asaiah went to Huldah the prophetess, the wife of Shallum the son of Tikvah, the son of Harhas, keeper of the wardrobe. (She dwelt in Jerusalem in the Second Quarter.) And they spoke with her. Then she said to them, "Thus says the LORD God of Israel, 'Tell the man who sent you to Me, "Thus says the LORD: 'Behold, I will bring calamity on this place and on its inhabitants—all the words of

> the book which the king of Judah has read—because they have forsaken Me and burned incense to other gods, that they might provoke Me to anger with all the works of their hands. Therefore My wrath shall be aroused against this place and shall not be quenched.' " ' But as for the king of Judah, who sent you to inquire of the LORD, in this manner you shall speak to him, 'Thus says the LORD God of Israel: "*Concerning* the words which you have heard—because your heart was tender, and you humbled yourself before the LORD when you heard what I spoke against this place and against its inhabitants, that they would become a desolation and a curse, and you tore your clothes and wept before Me, I also have heard *you,*" says the LORD. Surely, therefore, I will gather you to your fathers, and you shall be gathered to your grave in peace; and your eyes shall not see all the calamity which I will bring on this place." ' " So they brought back word to the king. (2 Kings 22:12–20)

The Lord in His mercy spares Josiah from judgment because Josiah was truly grieved over the sin of the nation. Josiah begins to purge Israel of idolatrous priests, high places, images, and even reinstates the Passover. The Scriptures summarize Josiah's life as follows.

> Now before him there was no king like him, who turned to the LORD with all his heart, with all his

> soul, and with all his might, according to all the Law of Moses; nor after him did *any* arise like him. (2 Kings 23:25)

Facing life with the Scriptures requires that you turn to the Lord with all your heart, soul, might, and mind. So how do we cultivate the kind of prayer, passion, and courage of Hannah, Daniel, and Josiah?

It begins with the right thoughts followed by the right actions. Let me express this as a formula:

information + application = sanctification
or
Bible + obedience = godliness

Real change through prayer happens when godly thoughts join godly actions. Consider memorizing the following passages to help you face life with the Scriptures.

Thinking

> Finally, brethren, whatever things are true, whatever things are noble, whatever things are just, whatever things are pure, whatever things are lovely, whatever things are of good report, if there is any virtue and if there is anything praiseworthy—meditate on these things. (Philippians 4:8)

Doing

> The things which you learned and received and heard and saw in me, these do, and the God of peace will be with you. (Philippians 4:9)

Asking

> Now this is the confidence that we have in Him, that if we ask anything according to His will, He hears us. (1 John 5:14)

Approaching

> For we do not have a High Priest who cannot sympathize with our weaknesses, but was in all *points* tempted as *we are, yet* without sin. Let us therefore come boldly to the throne of grace, that we may obtain mercy and find grace to help in time of need. (Hebrews 4:15–16)

Helping

> No temptation has overtaken you except such as is common to man; but God *is* faithful, who will not allow you to be tempted beyond what you are able, but with the temptation will also make the way of escape, that you may be able to bear *it.* (1 Corinthians 10:13)

I have found it helpful to study people in the Bible. Although we are separated by time and culture, circumstances surrounding sin remain the same. Train yourself to know the people in the Bible and how they responded to testing, sin, and temptation.

Whether they were successful or utterly failed, seek to learn from their experience.

I believe God is so sovereign that He can use your obedience or disobedience to accomplish His will and purposes. My prayer is He will use your obedience, rather than your disobedience. We must come to grips with the reality that we cannot fully glorify God through prayer unless His Truth is part of the prayer process and we face life obedient to the Scriptures.

PRAYER EXAMPLE

Arise, O Lord! Save me, O my God! (Psalm 3:7)

Lead me, Father, in Your righteousness because of my enemies. Show me the straight way to walk and give me more wisdom than Your enemies. (Psalm 5:8)

Father, the pain and suffering are too much to bear. I cannot live another day. I do not know how to hold on much longer. Help me, Father! (Job 1:20-22)

Help me to have hope in this trial. Let the suffering in my life accomplish its perfect work so that I am made perfect and complete. Let others see Jesus Christ through my suffering. I love You, Lord. (1 Peter 4:19)

YOUR PRAYER

CHAPTER SUMMARY

Step 3 – Face Life with the Scriptures

- **Hannah** (1 Samuel 10:4-11, 1 Samuel 2:1–10)
- **Daniel** (Daniel 2:14-23)
- **Josiah** (2 Kings 22:8-20)
- **information + application = sanctification**
- **Bible + obedience = godliness**
- **Thinking** (Philippians 4:8)
- **Doing** (Philippians 4:9)
- **Asking** (1 John 5:14)
- **Approaching** (Hebrews 4:15-16)
- **Helping** (1 Corinthians 10:13)

GROUP DISCUSSION

1. Share an experience with the group where a passage from the Scriptures helped you in a difficult time. Mention the passage and trial and the final outcome.

2. Have everyone in the group write anonymously on a separate paper a current situation in their life needing prayer. Have the leader collect these requests, and as a group talk through each one and identify a single Bible passage that would be applicable. Then pray through these as a group.

REFLECT THE GLORY OF GOD IN PRAYER

> Step 4

Love God & Love People

I thank my God upon every remembrance of you,
always in every prayer of mine making request for
you all with joy, for your fellowship in the gospel
from the first day until now,
being confident of this very thing,
that He who has begun a good work in you will
complete it until the day of Jesus Christ;
just as it is right for me to think this of you all,
because I have you in my heart, inasmuch as both in
my chains and in the defense and confirmation of
the gospel, you all are partakers with me of grace. For
God is my witness, how greatly I long for you all with
the affection of Jesus Christ. And this I pray,
that your love may abound still more and more in
knowledge and all discernment, that you may
approve the things that are excellent, that you may be
sincere and without offense till the day of Christ,
being filled with the fruits of righteousness which are
by Jesus Christ,
to the glory and praise of God.
Apostle Paul (Philippians 1:3–11)

Mirrors are helpful. They assist us in inspecting our outward appearance. They keep us and others safe while driving. There are even specialized mirrors to reveal blind spots around corners. In the last chapter we focused on facing life with the Scriptures, but life does not consist of viewing ourselves only. We can't remain in front of the mirror all day. Our gaze must extend upward and outward to fulfill our calling to love God and love people.

Imagine if tomorrow you were placed on the witness stand to prove you truly love God and others. With the courtroom cameras fixed upon you and all the world watching, what evidence could you submit that would withstand the scrutiny of an adversarial courtroom cross-examination?

△ STEP 4 △
LOVE GOD & LOVE PEOPLE

Jesus was cross-examined by unbelieving skeptics. He was once asked, "Teacher, which is the great commandment in the law?" His response, " '*You shall love the* LORD *your God with all your heart, with all your soul, and with all your mind.*' This is *the* first and great commandment. And *the* second *is* like it: '*You shall love your neighbor as yourself.*' On these two commandments hang all the Law and the Prophets." (Matthew 22:35–40)

Jesus loved His Father, and He loves people, even His enemies.

At the intersection of life and prayer is loving God and loving people. If we neglect to intercede on behalf of others, then we fail to truly love. The Bible uses a unique word for this kind of love, it is *agapao*. It is a love that is noble and sacrificial, rooted in the will rather than mere emotions. The Bible describes this kind of love in so many amazing ways. There is one particular passage about love in the Scriptures that is often quoted at weddings.

> Though I speak with the tongues of men and of angels, but have not love, I have become sounding brass or a clanging cymbal. And though I have the gift of prophecy, and understand all mysteries and all knowledge, and though I have all faith, so that I could remove mountains, but have not love, I am nothing. And though I bestow all my goods to feed the poor, and though I give my body to be burned, but have not love, it profits me nothing. Love suffers long and is kind; love does not envy; love does not parade itself, is not puffed up; does not behave rudely, does not seek its own, is not provoked, thinks no evil; does not rejoice in iniquity, but rejoices in the truth; bears all things, believes all things, hopes all things, endures all things. Love never fails. But whether there are prophecies, they will fail; whether there are

> tongues, they will cease; whether there is knowledge, it will vanish away. (1 Corinthians 13:1-8)

Jesus loves this way. His death on the cross is the greatest act of love of all time. Jesus, the only begotten Son of God, the unique God-Man, the perfect Lamb of God who takes away the sins of the world, loves God the Father by submitting to the Father's will to rescue and redeem rebellious sinners from the curse of the law and the wrath to come. Jesus perfectly obeys God's plan and purpose to pay the price and bear the full punishment for your sin. Jesus loves others and you by being your substitute for sin, taking your place of punishment, and cancelling out your certificate of debt that is hostile to you. Christ died for your sins according to the Scriptures; He was buried and He rose again the third day according to the Scriptures. Jesus loves God. Jesus loves you. This love is rooted in loving truth and is revealed by loving people sacrificially. This is the Gospel! Do you believe it?

Question: Have you confessed with your mouth that Jesus is Lord and believed in your heart that God has raised Him from the dead? Has your faith in Christ and trusting in His righteousness resulted in you loving God and loving people?

Loving Truth

Today, people are defining truth for themselves. Expressions such as "if it is true to you, then it is true" capture the sentiment that truth is relative and not absolute. It communicates the belief that 'truth' resides in the individual rather than being outside the individual, transcendent of time and culture. This is a dangerous precedent and encourages the idea that you can remove 'truth' by removing the individual. We need to pray that people will realize truth is found in God and not men. For men can only discover and affirm what has been established as true by God.

The longest psalm in the Bible is Psalm 119 and it is about God's truth. The psalmist expresses repeatedly his love for God's law.

> Oh, how I love Your law! It *is* my meditation all the day. (Psalm 119:97)

> I hate the double-minded, But I love Your law. (Psalm 119:113)

> I hate and abhor lying, *But* I love Your law. (Psalm 119:163)

These texts reveal that there are timeless, transcendent, unchanging truths whose origins reside with God and not man. Without absolute truths, eventually, there will be chaos and conflict.

For example, imagine four cars arriving at the same intersection at the same time and each driver interpreting the meaning and truth of the colored lights differently from one another. There will be confusion, crashes, and causalities. Fortunately, most people obey the rules of the road as prescribed in the law, and as a result, our roads are generally safe for travel. But if you look at any conflict at the international, national, local, and even family level, you discover that each side in the conflict is believing their interpretation of the facts is true and correct.

Question: How can such conflicts be resolved when compromise and concession are not possible? How can seemingly irreconcilable differences be overcome, when facts and truths are in dispute?

Loving Sacrificially

Loving sacrificially is the first part of the answer. If you combine sacrificial love with loving truth, which can be difficult and even dangerous at times, you will discover something wonderful and delightful.

I recommend reading the biography of any missionary who exchanged the comforts of home for a foreign country in order to love strangers with the Gospel of Christ. Learn how these missionaries faced opposition when they proclaimed Jesus Christ and His Gospel. Some missionaries were persecuted and even killed by the very ones they loved with the truth of the Gospel. It is these kinds of sacrifices that provide you with a sense of the great cost of loving truth and loving sacrificially. I recommend researching Jim Elliot, William Carey, Mary Slessor, Amy Carmichael, Eric Liddell, and John Paton. Unfortunately, the beautiful union of loving truth and loving people sacrificially can easily be broken. What would you think of someone who believes he or she is right and true, but is willing to harm others over his or her beliefs? For example, a terrorist expresses hate and carries out acts of violence, all the while claiming to love some god and faithfulness to his or her tradition of truth. This is sacrificial hate, not sacrificial love.

The Apostle Paul was originally known as Saul. Before his Damascus road conversion led him to become a disciple of Jesus Christ, he sacrificially hated like a terrorist. He was involved in the stoning of Stephen, the first martyr of the early church. His hate toward others escalated as he persecuted followers of Jesus Christ by throwing them into jail, all along breathing threats and murder against all Christians.

But Jesus lovingly intervened, confronting and forgiving Paul's sin. Paul repented and believed in Jesus Christ for the salvation of his soul. Listen to the words of the Apostle Paul regarding this experience.

> And the grace of our Lord was exceedingly abundant, with faith and love which are in Christ Jesus. This is a faithful saying and worthy of all acceptance, that Christ Jesus came into the world to save sinners, of whom I am chief. However, for

> this reason I obtained mercy, that in me first Jesus Christ might show all longsuffering, as a pattern to those who are going to believe on Him for everlasting life. Now to the King eternal, immortal, invisible, to God who alone is wise, be honor and glory forever and ever. Amen." (1 Timothy 1:14–17)

Question: How could such a transformation take place? Can people who are this violent change?

The answer is a resounding yes, but such change will only be found in Jesus Christ. Consider the words of the Apostle Paul from his letter to the believers in Rome.

> For when we were still without strength, in due time Christ died for the ungodly. For scarcely for a righteous man will one die; yet perhaps for a good man someone would even dare to die. But God demonstrates His own love toward us, in that while we were still sinners, Christ died for us. Much more then, having now been justified by His blood, we shall be saved from wrath through Him. For if when we were enemies we were reconciled to God through the death of His Son, much more, having been reconciled, we shall be saved by His life. And not only that, but we also rejoice in God through our Lord Jesus Christ, through whom we have now received the reconciliation. (Romans 5:6–11)

Paul understood that Jesus Christ loves the truth and loves sacrificially. When Paul comprehended that he was an enemy of Jesus and yet, Jesus was willing to forgive his sin and love him (who was an enemy), the outcome was transformative.

Loving your enemy? Preposterous and impossible you say? The world's love is corrupted, fleshly, selfish, and short-lived, but the God of the Bible does not love like the world. God makes known His own love toward us in that while we were yet sinners, Christ died for us.

The world does not know this kind of love from God, but they desperately need this kind of love. Paul was sent forth to love like Christ and he suffered much in this mission; but he had contentment, thanksgiving, and even offered praise to God Almighty. Christian, you must do likewise.

Question: How can I love and pray for those who hate me, hate the truth of the Bible, and hate my Savior? How can I love like Christ, or like the Apostle Paul?

I believe more of the answer is found, tucked away in a short passage in the letter to the Philippians.

> Let this mind be in you which was also in Christ Jesus, who, being in the form of God, did not consider it robbery to be equal with God, but made Himself of no reputation, taking the form of a bondservant, and coming in the likeness of

> men. And being found in appearance as a man, He humbled Himself and became obedient to the point of death, even the death of the cross. Therefore God also has highly exalted Him and given Him the name which is above every name, that at the name of Jesus every knee should bow, of those in heaven, and of those on earth, and of those under the earth, and that every tongue should confess that Jesus Christ is Lord, to the glory of God the Father. (Philippians 2:5–11)

This passage reveals the attitudes and actions of Jesus Christ on why and how He loves truth, God, and people sacrificially. This passage reveals that Jesus is God. He shares the same nature as God the Father. Yet, Jesus willingly chose to function in submission to God the Father. This submission came with a cost. It required the humiliation of becoming a lowly man to save and serve sinners, even his enemies. It required the disgrace and dishonor of a public execution by crucifixion—a humiliating, utterly painful, and tortuous death. All the while, He was sinless, innocent, and undeserving of such punishment.

Question: In this passage, why does God the Father honor and exalt Jesus? Why should everyone, everywhere bow down and confess Jesus as Lord?

The answer is simple: no one was more humble in attitude and action in loving truth, loving God, and loving people. This was the greatest sacrifice of all time. Remember in His crucifixion, Jesus Christ, the Lamb of God, took away the sins of the world, and God's wrath fell upon Him alone. We require a Savior and rescue from our sin. Jesus is worthy of our worship.

So how do we apply such amazing truths? Let me illustrate. Imagine Jesus Christ at the top of your stairs. He is God in heaven. He comes all the way down the steps to you on earth and serves you. He crosses the infinite gap between Creator and creature. He humbles Himself to die in your place as your substitute in order to make full payment for your sin with His life. The implications of this truth could be summarized as follows:

Without humility there can be no reconciliation.

Had Christ not humbled Himself, you would still be dead in your sins, unable to pay for your sins, and unreconciled to God as an enemy of God. You would be without hope in this world, awaiting final judgment for your sin in the lake of fire, originally created by God for the Devil and disobedient angels.

But if you humble yourself, confess your sin, repent (turn from your sin and dead works), believe in Jesus, and trust in Him alone as your substitute and sacrifice for sin, then God will forgive you, exchange your sin debt for Christ's righteousness, and adopt you permanently into His family. As a child of God, you will receive the Holy Spirit so that you can live a life loving and obeying the truths of the Scriptures, loving God, and loving people.

From this foundation, in prayer and by the power of the Holy Spirit, submitting to the truth of the Scriptures, you are to go forth. You go into the world with humility, denying yourself, carrying the cross of Christ, and using all your time, talents, and treasures for the proclamation of the Gospel of Christ so that others can hear and see the Gospel of Christ in word and in deed. You witness and evangelize as an ambassador for Christ, always pleading with others to be reconciled to God with the hope and prayer they will repent and believe the message of the Gospel.

This leaves no room for idleness or pride, does it? Considering the infinite distance traversed by Christ the Creator to reach you, His creature, and in light of the finite distance between you and others, is it too much to reach out to those you know with the Gospel? Can you understand why God is opposed to the proud? May you and I never, ever be unwilling in any moment for a friend or foe to go any distance in humility to share the Gospel. Do not withhold from anyone the saving knowledge of the truth of the Scriptures and the love of God.

And remember, as you go forth as a living sacrifice, memorize and hold close these wonderful promises in the Scriptures:

> For I am persuaded that neither death nor life, nor angels nor principalities nor powers, nor things present nor things to come, nor height nor depth, nor any other created thing, shall be able to separate us from the love of God which is in Christ Jesus our Lord. (Romans 8:38–39)

If we are to reflect the glory of God in prayer, then let us love truth, love God, and love people sacrificially.

Question: Have you failed at loving God and loving others? Do you struggle to love sacrificially?

First Love

Do you remember in Revelation 2:1-7 how Jesus rebuked the church in Ephesus?

> Nevertheless I have this against you, that you have left your first love. (Revelation 2:4)

How sad it must have been that day for the believers when the letter arrived, and they read the strong reprimand for leaving their first love of Christ. How could this have happened? It seems almost unimaginable, especially knowing that years earlier Paul wrote to the young Ephesian church and mentioned the need to love nearly 20 times. Have you left your first love? What a serious and sober warning to each of us.

To ensure loving God is your priority, examine your prayer life. Are you neglecting to love God in prayer? Do you praise Him, thank Him, and ask Him for help daily? Ask God to help you persevere in loving Him with sincerity. Ask Him to help you love people in a tangible, sacrificial way.

Question: How do we examine ourselves to ensure we are rightly loving God and others? Are you familiar with the test given by the Apostle John in 1 John 3:17-18?

Test: Loving Others

> But whoever has this world's goods, and sees his brother in need, and shuts up his heart from him, how does the love of God abide in him? My little children, let us not love in word or in tongue, but in deed and in truth. (1 John 3:17–18)

Question: Are you seeing and meeting the needs of others? Are you loving in deed and in truth?

Below is a list of passages on loving others. By no means is this list exhaustive of all the Bible speaks on this topic. Please read, mediate, memorize, and apply.

> For you, brethren, have been called to liberty; only do not use liberty as an opportunity for the flesh,

but through love serve one another. For all the law is fulfilled in one word, even in this: "You shall love your neighbor as yourself." But if you bite and devour one another, beware lest you be consumed by one another! I say then: Walk in the Spirit, and you shall not fulfill the lust of the flesh. (Galatians 5:13–16)

We are bound to thank God always for you, brethren, as it is fitting, because your faith grows exceedingly, and the love of every one of you all abounds toward each other (2 Thessalonians 1:3)

Let brotherly love continue. Do not forget to entertain strangers, for by so doing some have unwittingly entertained angels. Remember the prisoners as if chained with them—those who are mistreated—since you yourselves are in the body also. (Hebrews 13:1–3)

Since you have purified your souls in obeying the truth through the Spirit in sincere love of the brethren, love one another fervently with a pure heart (1 Peter 1:22)

By this we know love, because He laid down His life for us. And we also ought to lay down our lives for the brethren. (1 John 3:16)

As you journey through life to live and love, there will be challenges and conflicts. In these moments especially be in prayer. The Psalms have countless examples of souls crying out to God in prayer.

> Give ear to my words, O LORD, Consider my meditation. Give heed to the voice of my cry, My King and my God, For to You I will pray. My voice You shall hear in the morning, O LORD; In the morning I will direct it to You, And I will look up. For You are not a God who takes pleasure in wickedness, Nor shall evil dwell with You. (Psalm 5:1–4)

May you relish your time of private prayer with your Creator and Savior and fan the flames of love for God's truth, God Himself, and people. Remember, knowledge alone will puff up and harden the heart. But serving and sacrificing in truth for God and others, creates a heart of compassion and opportunity for prayer.

PRAYER EXAMPLE

I love you Lord. You saved me and redeemed me. I should be dead and in hell, but you spared me. You delivered me from drugs and alcohol. Thank you, Father.

I love my wife. I love my children. Thank you for each one of them. You knew Father that it was best that I should not be alone, and you have blessed me with a wonderful family. Thank you! May you continue your work in each of them, so their life and talents bring great glory to you.

I pray for those attending Brookside Baptist Church. Grow them Lord to be pillars in your Church. May they be salt and light in the community as they share the Gospel to those they encounter. Help each one of them to have victory in their walk with you. Bless their efforts to honor and serve you. Keep them holy. Protect them Father from the Evil One.

YOUR PRAYER

CHAPTER SUMMARY

Step 4 – Loving God and Loving People

- **Defining Love (**1 Corinthians 13:1-8)
- **Loving Truth** (Psalm 119:97, 113, 163)
- **Loving Sacrificially (**Romans 5:6–11)
- **Without humility there can be no reconciliation** (Philippians 2:5-11)
- **First Love** (Revelation 2:1-7)
- **Test: Loving Others** (1 John 3:17–18)

GROUP DISCUSSION

1. Share with one another examples of Christ's tangible love for you.

2. Think back to a moment when someone loved you sacrificially. What did it feel like? How did you respond?

3. Make a list of specific individuals who you know need salvation and pray for them as a group.

4. Make a list of several individuals who require a tangible expression of Christ's love. Determine how the group might meet some of these needs in the next seven days, or before you meet again.

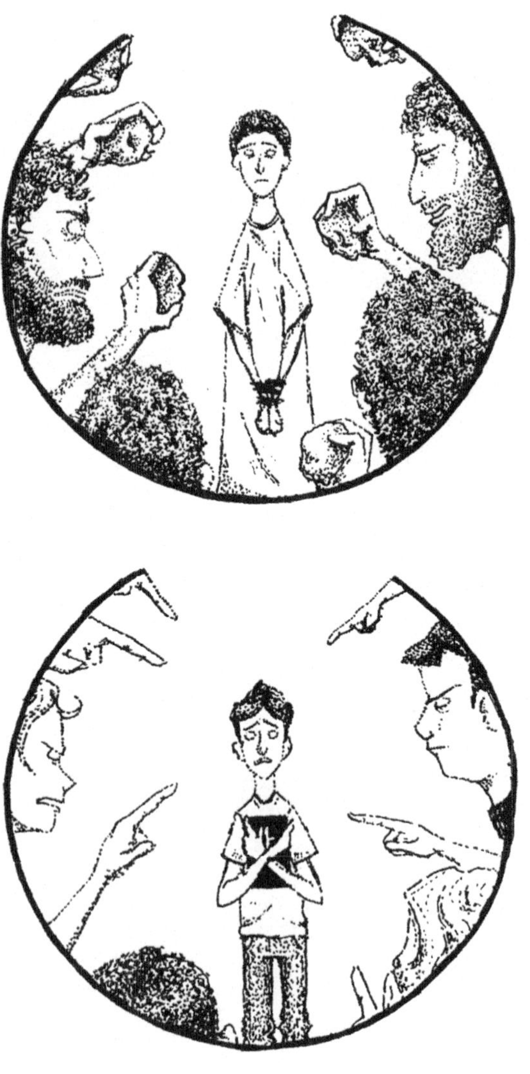

> Step 5

Expect Suffering & Persecution

And when they had come to the place called Calvary,
there they crucified Him, and the criminals,
one on the right hand and the other on the left.

Then Jesus said, "Father, forgive them,
for they do not know what they do."

And they divided His garments and cast lots.
And the people stood looking on.
But even the rulers with them sneered, saying,
"He saved others; let Him save Himself if He is the
Christ, the chosen of God."
The soldiers also mocked Him,
coming and offering Him sour wine, and saying,
"If You are the King of the Jews, save Yourself."
And an inscription also was written over Him in
letters of Greek, Latin, and Hebrew:
THIS IS THE KING OF THE JEWS
Jesus Christ (Luke 23:33-38)

Christian history is awash with instances of followers of Christ suffering persecution for the sake of the Gospel. In Hebrews chapter 11, we learn about those who suffered prior to the cross for faith in God.

Alongside these witnesses, there is an untold number of faithful men, women, and children of whom the world is not worthy, who persevered and prayed under the most difficult circumstances of suffering and persecution for a real hope and a Savior they could not see. But why does persecution happen?

> **Yes, and all who desire to live godly in Christ Jesus will suffer persecution. (2 Timothy 3:12)**

When we live as lights, faithful and obedient to the truth of the Scriptures, following Jesus Christ's word and example, we should not be surprised when the world rejects us. But if we do not properly prepare ourselves in prayer for suffering and persecution, we may undermine the very Gospel we are proclaiming.

Question: What prayer would you pray if you were persecuted? Are you willing to suffer for the Gospel?

△ STEP 5 △
EXPECT SUFFERING & PERSECUTION

Instructions

Let us take a different approach in this chapter. I would like for you to simply read the selected Biblical accounts of various individuals who experienced persecution or suffering. There is room after each story for you to jot down any thoughts about the context and content of their prayer that made an impression on you. If something appears remarkable, shocking, challenging, wonderful, or applicable for your life, make a note about the details that are important and relevant. You may wish to share your thoughts with others, especially if you are taking part in a small group study.

While you are reflecting on the actions and attitudes of these faithful souls, ask the Lord for the courage and conviction to live wholly to Christ and His Word regardless of the cost to you in this life.

Stephen: First Christian Martyr

> When they heard these things they were cut to the heart, and they gnashed at him with their teeth. But he, being full of the Holy Spirit, gazed into heaven and saw the glory of God, and Jesus standing at the right hand of God, and said, "Look! I see the heavens opened and the Son of Man standing at the right hand of God!" Then they cried out with a loud voice, stopped their

ears, and ran at him with one accord; and they cast him out of the city and stoned him. And the witnesses laid down their clothes at the feet of a young man named Saul. And they stoned Stephen as he was calling on God and saying, "Lord Jesus, receive my spirit." Then he knelt down and cried out with a loud voice, "Lord, do not charge them with this sin." And when he had said this, he fell asleep. (Acts 7:54–60)

Paul: Suffering for the Gospel

Are they Hebrews? So am I. Are they Israelites? So am I. Are they the seed of Abraham? So am I. Are they ministers of Christ?—I speak as a fool—I am more: in labors more abundant, in stripes above measure, in prisons more frequently, in deaths often. From the Jews five times I received forty stripes minus one. Three times I was beaten with rods; once I was stoned; three times I was shipwrecked; a night and a day I have been in the deep; in journeys often, in perils of waters, in perils of robbers, in perils of my own countrymen, in perils of the Gentiles, in perils in the city, in perils in the wilderness, in perils in the sea, in perils among false brethren; in weariness and toil, in sleeplessness often, in hunger and thirst, in fastings often, in cold and nakedness—besides the other things, what comes upon me daily: my deep concern for all the churches. Who is weak, and I am not weak? Who is made to stumble, and I do not burn with indignation? If I must boast, I will boast in the things which concern my infirmity. The God and Father of our Lord Jesus Christ, who is blessed forever, knows that I am not lying. In Damascus the governor, under Aretas the king, was guarding the city of the Damascenes with a garrison, desiring to arrest me; (2 Corinthians 11:22–32)

Job: Satanic Attack

Now there was a day when his sons and daughters were eating and drinking wine in their oldest brother's house; and a messenger came to Job and said, "The oxen were plowing and the donkeys feeding beside them, when the Sabeans raided them and took them away—indeed they have killed the servants with the edge of the sword; and I alone have escaped to tell you!" While he was still speaking, another also came and said, "The fire of God fell from heaven and burned up the sheep and the servants, and consumed them; and I alone have escaped to tell you!" While he was still speaking, another also came and said, "The Chaldeans formed three bands, raided the camels and took them away, yes, and killed the servants with the edge of the sword; and I alone have escaped to tell you!" While he was still speaking, another also came and said, "Your sons and daughters were eating and drinking wine in their oldest brother's house, and suddenly a great wind came from across the wilderness and struck the four corners of the house, and it fell on the young people, and they are dead; and I alone have escaped to tell you!" Then Job arose, tore his robe, and shaved his head; and he fell to the ground and worshiped. And he said: "Naked I came from my mother's womb, And naked shall I return there. The LORD gave, and the LORD has taken away; Blessed be the name of the LORD." In all this Job did not sin nor charge God with wrong. Again there was a day when the sons of God came to present themselves before the LORD, and Satan came also among them to present himself before the LORD. And the LORD said to Satan, "From where do you come?" Satan answered the LORD and said, "From going to and fro on the earth, and from walking back and forth on it." Then the LORD said to Satan, "Have you considered My servant Job, that there is none like him on the earth, a blameless and upright man, one who fears God and shuns evil? And still he holds fast to his integrity, although you incited Me against him, to destroy him without cause." So Satan answered the LORD and said, "Skin for skin! Yes, all that a man has he will give for his life. But stretch out Your hand now, and touch his bone and his flesh, and he will surely curse You to Your face!" And the LORD said to Satan, "Behold, he is in your hand, but spare his life." So Satan went out from the presence of the LORD, and struck Job with painful boils from the sole of his foot to the crown of his head. And he took for himself a potsherd with which to scrape himself while he sat in the midst of the ashes. Then his wife said to him, "Do you still hold fast to your integrity? Curse God and die!" But he said to her, "You speak as one of the foolish women speaks. Shall we indeed accept good from God, and shall we not accept adversity?" In all this Job did not sin with his lips. (Job 1:13–2:10)

Daniel's Three Friends: You will Surely Burn

There are certain Jews whom you have set over the affairs of the province of Babylon: Shadrach, Meshach, and Abed-Nego; these men, O king, have not paid due regard to you. They do not serve your gods or worship the gold image which you have set up." Then Nebuchadnezzar, in rage and fury, gave the command to bring Shadrach,

Meshach, and Abed-Nego. So they brought these men before the king. Nebuchadnezzar spoke, saying to them, "Is it true, Shadrach, Meshach, and Abed-Nego, that you do not serve my gods or worship the gold image which I have set up? Now if you are ready at the time you hear the sound of the horn, flute, harp, lyre, and psaltery, in symphony with all kinds of music, and you fall down and worship the image which I have made, good! But if you do not worship, you shall be cast immediately into the midst of a burning fiery furnace. And who is the god who will deliver you from my hands?" Shadrach, Meshach, and Abed-Nego answered and said to the king, "O Nebuchadnezzar, we have no need to answer you in this matter. If that is the case, our God whom we serve is able to deliver us from the burning fiery furnace, and He will deliver us from your hand, O king. But if not, let it be known to you, O king, that we do not serve your gods, nor will we worship the gold image which you have set up." Then Nebuchadnezzar was full of fury, and the expression on his face changed toward Shadrach, Meshach, and Abed-Nego. He spoke and commanded that they heat the furnace seven times more than it was usually heated. And he commanded certain mighty men of valor who were in his army to bind Shadrach, Meshach, and Abed-Nego, and cast them into the burning fiery furnace. Then these men were bound in their coats, their trousers, their turbans, and their other garments, and were cast into the midst of the burning fiery furnace. Therefore, because the king's command was urgent, and the furnace exceedingly hot, the flame of the fire killed those men who took up Shadrach, Meshach, and Abed-Nego. And these three men, Shadrach, Meshach, and Abed-Nego, fell down bound into the midst of the burning fiery furnace. Then King Nebuchadnezzar was astonished; and he rose in haste and spoke, saying to his counselors, "Did we not cast three men bound into the midst of the fire?" They answered and said to the king, "True, O king." "Look!" he answered, "I see four men loose, walking in the midst of the fire; and they are not hurt, and the form of the fourth is like the Son of God." Then Nebuchadnezzar went near the mouth of the burning fiery furnace and spoke, saying, "Shadrach, Meshach, and Abed-Nego, servants of the Most High God, come out, and come here." Then Shadrach, Meshach, and Abed-Nego came from the midst of the fire. And the satraps, administrators, governors, and the king's counselors gathered together, and they saw these men on whose bodies the fire had no power; the hair of their head was not singed nor were their garments affected, and the smell of fire was not on them. Nebuchadnezzar spoke, saying, "Blessed be the God of Shadrach, Meshach, and Abed-Nego, who sent His Angel and delivered His servants who trusted in Him, and they have frustrated the king's word, and yielded their bodies, that they should not serve nor worship any god except their own God! Therefore I make a decree that any people, nation, or language which speaks anything amiss against the God of Shadrach, Meshach, and Abed-Nego shall be cut in pieces, and their houses shall be made an ash heap; because there is no other God who can deliver like this." Then the king promoted Shadrach, Meshach, and Abed-Nego in the province of Babylon. (Daniel 3:12–30)

Nehemiah: Silent Prayer

O Lord, I pray, please let Your ear be attentive to the prayer of Your servant, and to the prayer of Your servants who desire to fear Your name; and let Your servant prosper this day, I pray, and grant him mercy in the sight of this man." For I was the king's cupbearer. And it came to pass in the month of Nisan, in the twentieth year of King Artaxerxes, when wine was before him, that I took the wine and gave it to the king. Now I had never been sad in his presence before. Therefore the king said to me, "Why is your face sad, since you are not sick? This is nothing but sorrow of heart." So I became dreadfully afraid, and said to the king, "May the king live forever! Why should my face not be sad, when the city, the place of my fathers' tombs, lies waste, and its gates are burned with fire?" Then the king said to me, "What do you request?" So I prayed to the God of heaven. And I said to the king, "If it pleases the king, and if your servant has found favor in your sight, I ask that you send me to Judah, to the city of my fathers' tombs, that I may rebuild it." Then the king said to me (the queen also sitting beside him), "How long will your journey be? And when will you return?" So it pleased the king to send me; and I set him a time. Furthermore I said to the king, "If it pleases the king, let letters be given to me for the governors of the region beyond the River, that they must permit me to pass through till I come to Judah, and a letter to Asaph the keeper of the king's forest, that he must give me timber to make beams for the gates of the citadel which pertains to the temple, for the city wall, and for the house that I will occupy." And the king granted them to me according to the good hand of my God upon me. (Nehemiah 1:11–2:8)

Paul & Silas: Jail Prayer

Then the multitude rose up together against them; and the magistrates tore off their clothes and commanded them to be beaten with rods. And when they had laid many stripes on them, they threw them into prison, commanding the jailer to keep them securely. Having received such a charge, he put them into the inner prison and fastened their feet in the stocks. But at midnight Paul and Silas were praying and singing hymns to God, and the prisoners were listening to them. Suddenly there was a great earthquake, so that the foundations of the prison were shaken; and immediately all the doors were opened and everyone's chains were loosed. And the keeper of the prison, awaking from sleep and seeing the prison doors open, supposing the prisoners had fled, drew his sword and was about to kill himself. But Paul called with a loud voice, saying, "Do yourself no harm, for we are all here." Then he called for a light, ran in, and fell down trembling before Paul and Silas. And he brought them out and said, "Sirs, what must I do to be saved?" So they said, "Believe on the Lord Jesus Christ, and you will be saved, you and your household." Then they spoke the word of the Lord to him and to all who were in his house. And he took them the same hour of the night and washed their stripes. And immediately he and all his family were baptized. Now when he had brought them into his house, he set food before them; and he rejoiced, having believed in God with all his household. And when it was day, the magistrates sent the officers, saying, "Let those men go." So the keeper of the prison reported these words to Paul, saying, "The magistrates have sent to let you go. Now therefore depart, and go in peace." But Paul said to them, "They have beaten us openly, uncondemned Romans, and have thrown us into prison. And now do they put us out secretly? No indeed! Let them come themselves and get us out." And the officers told these words to the magistrates, and they were afraid when they heard that they were Romans. Then they came and pleaded with them and brought them out, and asked them to depart from the city. So they went out of the prison and entered the house of Lydia; and when they had seen the brethren, they encouraged them and departed. (Acts 16:22–40)

Jesus Christ: Obeying God's Will

Then Jesus came with them to a place called Gethsemane, and said to the disciples, "Sit here while I go and pray over there." And He took with Him Peter and the two sons of Zebedee, and He began to be sorrowful and deeply distressed. Then He said to them, "My soul is exceedingly sorrowful, even to death. Stay here and watch with Me." He went a little farther and fell on His face, and prayed, saying, "O My Father, if it is

> possible, let this cup pass from Me; nevertheless, not as I will, but as You will." Then He came to the disciples and found them sleeping, and said to Peter, "What! Could you not watch with Me one hour? Watch and pray, lest you enter into temptation. The spirit indeed is willing, but the flesh is weak." Again, a second time, He went away and prayed, saying, "O My Father, if this cup cannot pass away from Me unless I drink it, Your will be done." And He came and found them asleep again, for their eyes were heavy. So He left them, went away again, and prayed the third time, saying the same words. (Matthew 26:36–44)

You: Will you Pray?

> But I say to you, love your enemies, bless those who curse you, do good to those who hate you, and pray for those who spitefully use you and persecute you, that you may be sons of your Father in heaven; for He makes His sun rise on the evil and on the good, and sends rain on the just and on the unjust. For if you love those who love you, what reward have you? Do not even the tax collectors do the same? And if you greet your brethren only, what do you do more than others? Do not even the tax collectors do so? Therefore

> you shall be perfect, just as your Father in heaven is perfect. (Matthew 5:44–48)

Trials and temptations are ALWAYS reasons to pray, but NEVER reasons to disobey.

Life is full of tests designed not to fail you but to refine you. By praying daily, you will be prepared to walk in the Spirit rather than the flesh, ready to accept and expect suffering and persecution.

Question: What is the role of prayer at the beginning, middle, and end of each day? Do you have an established routine of praying regularly?

In closing, denying yourself, carrying your cross, and following Christ in suffering for the sake of the Gospel pleases God and is rewardable at the judgment seat of Christ. Therefore, consider memorizing the following two passages to grow and respond prayerfully in faith.

Memorize Now

> Who shall separate us from the love of Christ? Shall tribulation, or distress, or persecution, or famine, or nakedness, or peril, or sword? As it is written: "For Your sake we are killed all day long;

> We are accounted as sheep for the slaughter." Yet in all these things we are more than conquerors through Him who loved us. For I am persuaded that neither death nor life, nor angels nor principalities nor powers, nor things present nor things to come, nor height nor depth, nor any other created thing, shall be able to separate us from the love of God which is in Christ Jesus our Lord. (Romans 8:35–39)

> Therefore, whether you eat or drink, or whatever you do, do all to the glory of God. (1 Corinthians 10:31)

Memorize Later

Use the following space to write down one other passage to encourage your walk in the Lord.

____

____

____

____

____

____

____

PRAYER EXAMPLE

Father give me strength and patience when others ridicule you. Help me to remember Your Word and what to say in difficult situations.

Help me to love the one persecuting me. Help me to show the love of Christ to them when they attack me because of you.

YOUR PRAYER

I pray for these lost souls:

CHAPTER SUMMARY

Step 5 – Expect Suffering & Persecution

- **Stephen** (Acts 7:54-60)
- **Paul** (2 Corinthians 11:22-32)
- **Job** (Job 1:13-2:10)
- **Daniel's Three Friends** (Daniel 3:12-30)
- **Nehemiah** (Nehemiah 1:11-2:8)
- **Paul & Silas** (Acts 16:22-40)
- **Jesus Christ** (Matthew 26:36-44)
- **You: Will you Pray?** (Matthew 5:44-48)

GROUP DISCUSSION

1. Who in the Bible encourages you in your walk in the Lord? Why?

2. Discuss what is holding you back from being more obedient to Christ and His Word?

3. When you think of suffering and persecution for the Gospel, what are some of the fears that come to mind?

4. Have you ever suffered for the Gospel? Are you thankful? What was the outcome or lesson learned?

5. What steps can you take today to prepare yourself to love those who may persecute you?

REFLECT THE GLORY OF GOD IN PRAYER

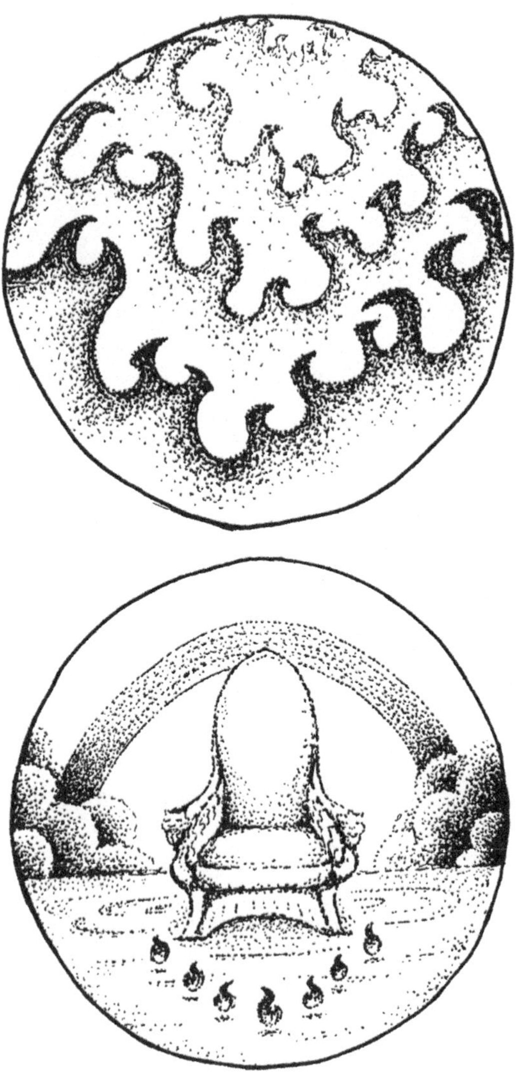

> Step 6

Concern Yourself with God's Kingdom

Continue earnestly in prayer,
being vigilant in it with thanksgiving;
meanwhile praying also for us,
that God would open to us a door for the word,
to speak the mystery of Christ,
for which I am also in chains, that I may make it
manifest, as I ought to speak. Walk in wisdom
toward those who are outside, redeeming the time.
Let your speech always be with grace,
seasoned with salt, that you may know
how you ought to answer each one.
The Apostle Paul (Colossians 4:2–6)

The year was 1998. It had been 3 years since I repented and put my faith in Jesus Christ for the forgiveness of my sin and salvation of my soul. It was nearing Christmas, and I had recently reached out to my father to discuss our family's plan to visit. Our conversation moved to the Gospel of Jesus Christ and what role our works played in the salvation of our souls. My dad replied, "Son, as long as your good works outweigh your bad works, 51% to 49%, you go to heaven."

I responded to my father, "Dad you are not saved by works, but by faith alone in Jesus alone. It is a free gift, not earned by works. Did you know the Bible answers this question directly? Let me share with you my favorite verse in the Scriptures, Ephesians 2:8-9. 'For by grace you have been saved through faith, and that not of yourselves, it is the gift of God, not as a result of works.' God says you are saved by grace, not by works." My father's response to God's Word still echoes in my head to this very day, "I don't believe it." The conversation ended shortly thereafter. Heartbroken, I thought to myself, "He rejected the Gospel. What do I do now?"

At once, I shared with my wife the conversation and we wept and prayed. We asked God to open another door of opportunity when we visit my dad the following week. After we finished praying, I remarked, "This situation needs prayer and fasting."

The next morning, I started to fast and pray for my father's salvation, and asked God for another opportunity to share the Gospel over the Christmas holiday. Later in the day, I received a call from my sister. She was crying. She revealed that dad had just died that morning.

In that moment, the world went silent. I could not hear anything. I then prayed to God, and said, "Lord, this is not what I had in mind when I set out to fast and pray! What in the world are You doing?" After I got off the phone with my sister, and told my wife, I ended my fast and just sat there replaying over and over in my mind my last conversation with my dad.

As the funeral arrangements came together, my dad had requested before his death that I give his eulogy at the funeral. It was at this moment I realized an important truth about prayer:

Prayer is NOT about me changing the mind of God, but God changing my mind; preparing me to obey His will.

In my grief, my narrow focus over the death and loss of my father kept me from seeing the wider vision of those who are living and would attend the funeral. My unbelieving family, cousins, friends of the family, neighbors, and the Catholic priest would have an opportunity to hear the Gospel. Praying to God changed my perspective and gave me a love and concern for others. God answered my prayer on the day of the funeral and gave me the concern and courage to proclaim the Gospel of Jesus Christ so they would know how to enter the kingdom of God.

△ STEP 6 △
CONCERN YOURSELF WITH GOD'S KINGDOM

Life, Death, and Judgment

The Scriptures say in Hebrews 9:27, "And as it is appointed for men to die once, but after this the judgment." Every single soul will die and come face to face with God their Maker as their final Judge. There are only two ultimate outcomes before the all-knowing and all-powerful Judge: condemned to the lake of fire for eternity or pardoned to the new heaven and new earth for eternity. The one who believes in this life in Christ is not condemned; but the one who does not believe in this life is condemned already, because they have not believed in Jesus, the only begotten Son of God (John 3:17–18).

Knowing that one's eternal destiny hinges on hearing and responding to the Gospel before death, should move and motivate every blood-bought, born-again believer to reach out to parents, siblings, cousins, friends, neighbors, unsaved religious individuals, and even strangers with the Good News of Jesus Christ. This is priority number one. This is mission number one. This is the Great Commission.

Authority & the Authorized Message

In Matthew 28:16-20, Jesus reveals that all authority in heaven and on earth has been given to Him from God the Father to authorize a single message for salvation. Any other message for salvation is not authorized. This is why Jesus unapologetically declares that He is the way, the truth, and the life and that no one comes to God the Father in heaven except through Him (John 14:6). The Apostle Paul stresses the one-and-only-way message of the Gospel with a severe warning in Galatians 1:8, "But even if we, or an angel from heaven, preach any other gospel to you than what we have preached to you, let him be accursed." To proclaim or claim there is another way to God is treasonous.

Knowing that people are facing eternal judgment and knowing there are false gospels and false teachers misleading people; we must be concerned about God's kingdom. When we are callous to the concerns of God's kingdom, we risk the chastening of God. I recommend reading chapters 2 and 3 of Revelation to understand Jesus Christ's concerns when His Church is off mission.

To help you pray with passion and priority in your concern for God's kingdom, please read and meditate on the following passages. Write down specific prayer requests for kingdom concerns where you live, work, and worship.

Kingdom's Work - Praying for Open Doors

> Meanwhile praying also for us, that God would open to us a door for the word, to speak the mystery of Christ, for which I am also in chains. (Colossians 4:3)

What doors do you need God to open in your community for a Gospel presentation? Be specific.

____

____

> and for me, that utterance may be given to me, that I may open my mouth boldly to make known the mystery of the gospel. (Ephesians 6:19)

Ask God for courage to share the Gospel to the following people this week. List the names below (family, friends, neighbors, colleagues, strangers, etc.)

____

____

Kingdom's Workers - Praying for Help

> Therefore pray the Lord of the harvest to send out laborers into His harvest. (Matthew 9:38)

I will pray for the following three people in my local church to become laborers in the harvest.

____

____

> Finally, brethren, pray for us, that the word of the Lord may run swiftly and be glorified, just as it is with you, and that we may be delivered from unreasonable and wicked men; for not all have faith. (2 Thessalonians 3:1–2)

I will pray for the following three people who are laboring in the harvest (local outreach, missionaries).

____

____

> "I pray for them. I do not pray for the world but for those whom You have given Me, for they are Yours. And all Mine are Yours, and Yours are Mine, and I am glorified in them. Now I am no longer in the world, but these are in the world, and I come to You. Holy Father, keep through Your name those whom You have given Me, that they may be one as We are. While I was with them in the world, I kept them in Your name. Those whom You gave Me I have kept; and none of them

> is lost except the son of perdition, that the Scripture might be fulfilled. But now I come to You, and these things I speak in the world, that they may have My joy fulfilled in themselves. I have given them Your word; and the world has hated them because they are not of the world, just as I am not of the world. I do not pray that You should take them out of the world, but that You should keep them from the evil one. They are not of the world, just as I am not of the world. Sanctify them by Your truth. Your word is truth. As You sent Me into the world, I also have sent them into the world. And for their sakes I sanctify Myself, that they also may be sanctified by the truth. "I do not pray for these alone, but also for those who will believe in Me through their word; (John 17:9–20)

I will pray for the following three people for protection from evil, and for growth in the knowledge of the Scriptures and obedience to the Truth.

Kingdom's Wayward - Praying for Unbelievers

> But I say to you, love your enemies, bless those who curse you, do good to those who hate you, and pray for those who spitefully use you and

> persecute you, that you may be sons of your Father in heaven; for He makes His sun rise on the evil and on the good, and sends rain on the just and on the unjust. For if you love those who love you, what reward have you? Do not even the tax collectors do the same? And if you greet your brethren only, what do you do more than others? Do not even the tax collectors do so? Therefore you shall be perfect, just as your Father in heaven is perfect. (Matthew 5:44–48)

I will pray for the salvation of the following three unbelievers. Ask God to help you find a way to love and do good for them in a tangible way.

> But you, beloved, building yourselves up on your most holy faith, praying in the Holy Spirit, keep yourselves in the love of God, looking for the mercy of our Lord Jesus Christ unto eternal life. And on some have compassion, making a distinction; but others save with fear, pulling them out of the fire, hating even the garment defiled by the flesh. Now to Him who is able to keep you from stumbling, And to present you faultless Before the presence of His glory with exceeding joy, To God our Savior, Who alone is

> wise, Be glory and majesty, Dominion and power, Both now and forever. Amen. (Jude 1:20–25)

Every day this week, ask God in prayer for one opportunity to show compassion to an unbeliever. Ask for wisdom to serve wisely. Describe below any opportunities seized or missed because of this prayer. Do not forget to be on alert and ready to act, regardless of the type of situation.

____

____

Before God delivered me from alcohol and drugs, I was pursuing self and sin to the ends of the world to build my kingdom with all my time, talents, and treasures. After God rescued me, He changed my heart and put in me a desire to pursue Him and His righteousness to the ends of the world to build His kingdom with all my time, talents, and treasures. Are you concerned about God's kingdom?

PRAYER EXAMPLE

Father, you know who is lost in my family. I pray you will open their eyes! Send other Christians into their lives to affirm your Gospel.

Lord God, I pray for the lost people at work and in my neighborhood.

Dearest Heavenly Father, I pray for the salvation of the strangers I met today. I do not know their names, but you do. Save them Father. Redeem them!

YOUR PRAYER

CHAPTER SUMMARY

Step 6 – Concern Yourself with God's Kingdom

- **Life, Death and Judgment** (Hebrews 9:27)
- **Authority & the Authorized Message** (Matthew 28:16-20)
- **Kingdom's Work - Praying for Open Doors** (Colossians 4:3, Ephesians 6:19)
- **Kingdom's Workers - Praying for Help** (Matthew 9:38, 2 Thessalonians 3:1-2, John 17:9-20)
- **Kingdom's Wayward - Praying for Unbelievers** (Matthew 5:44-48, Jude 1:20-25)

GROUP DISCUSSION

1. Make a list of reasons why you held back from sharing the Gospel. Discuss biblical and practical solutions to prevent this from happening again in the future.

2. Make a list of practical ways you and the church you attend can evangelize in the local community. Consider tracts, training, and other ideas for sharing the Gospel.

REFLECT THE GLORY OF GOD IN PRAYER

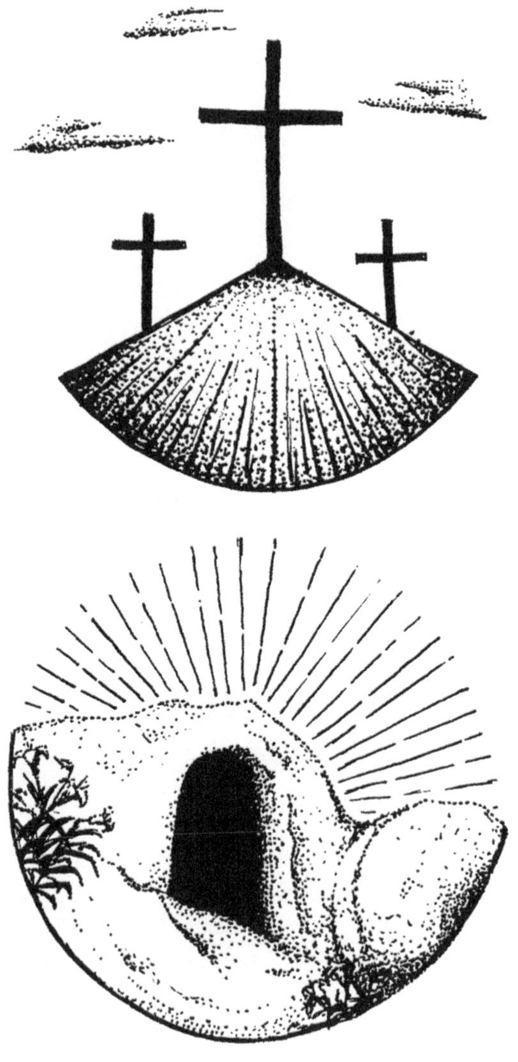

> Step 7

Take Every Opportunity

For this reason we also, since the day we heard it,
do not cease to pray for you,
and to ask that you may be filled with the knowledge
of His will in all wisdom and spiritual understanding;
that you may walk worthy of the Lord, fully pleasing
Him, being fruitful in every good work and
increasing in the knowledge of God; strengthened
with all might,
according to His glorious power,
for all patience and longsuffering with joy;
giving thanks to the Father who has qualified us to be
partakers of the inheritance of the saints in the light.
He has delivered us from the power of darkness and
conveyed us into the kingdom of the Son of His love,
in whom we have redemption through His blood,
the forgiveness of sins.
Apostle Paul (Colossians 1:9-14)

Pray without ceasing (1 Thessalonians 5:17). Do you remember the first time you read this command? As a new believer, encountering this truth, I thought to myself, "How in the world is that even possible? Sure, Jesus and Paul could pray unceasingly, but I am a mere babe in Christ." But in reading the Scriptures and talking to knowledgeable believers, it became clearer that there is a multitude of ways to pray. There is a formal prayer where you set aside time to pray in your "prayer closet"; there are prayers at meals, prayers at church and in Bible studies with other believers. But then I discovered that sharing your thoughts with God throughout the day can be a type of praying as well. My prayer life was revolutionized.

At any moment, you and I can pray to God the Father on His throne, through God the Son, Jesus Christ with the help of the Holy Spirit. Jesus is the only mediator between God and men, and as the only High Priest to God, is the only person who can hear and pass prayers directly to God the Father. God the Spirit or Holy Spirit, who permanently lives in true believers, assists us in our weakness because we do not always know how to pray as we should. The whole Trinity is involved in prayer! May the words of our mouth and the meditations of our heart be acceptable in Your sight, O Lord, our Rock, and Redeemer (Psalm 19:4).

△ STEP 7 △
TAKE EVERY OPPORTUNITY

If you follow through on all the previous steps of prayer but neglect to persevere in prayer by taking every opportunity, you will fall short, lose your joy and intimacy with God, find yourself inattentive to God's will, and powerless against the schemes of the devil. There is a strong warning in the Scriptures regarding the importance of being diligent in our faith.

Be Diligent

> But also for this very reason, giving all diligence, add to your faith virtue, to virtue knowledge, to knowledge self-control, to self-control perseverance, to perseverance godliness, to godliness brotherly kindness, and to brotherly kindness love. For if these things are yours and abound, you will be neither barren nor unfruitful in the knowledge of our Lord Jesus Christ. For he who lacks these things is shortsighted, even to blindness, and has forgotten that he was cleansed from his old sins. Therefore, brethren, be even more diligent to make your call and election sure, for if you do these things you will never stumble; for so an entrance will be supplied to you abundantly into the everlasting kingdom of our Lord and Savior Jesus Christ. (2 Peter 1:5–11)

Below are several passages to stimulate your thinking in several key areas of your Christian walk. Consider reading and praying through these Scriptures.

Remember Christ's Death, Burial, & Resurrection

> Moreover, brethren, I declare to you the gospel which I preached to you, which also you received and in which you stand, by which also you are saved, if you hold fast that word which I preached to you—unless you believed in vain. For I delivered to you first of all that which I also received: that Christ died for our sins according to the Scriptures, and that He was buried, and that He rose again the third day according to the Scriptures. (1 Corinthians 15:1–4)

Remember God's Forgiveness

> For He (God the Father) made Him (Jesus Christ) who knew no sin to be sin for us, that we might become the righteousness of God in Him. (2 Corinthians 5:21)

> And you, being dead in your trespasses and the uncircumcision of your flesh, He has made alive together with Him, having forgiven you all trespasses, having wiped out the handwriting of requirements that was against us, which was contrary to us. And He has taken it out of the way, having nailed it to the cross. (Colossians 2:13–14)

Be Thankful

in everything give thanks; for this is the will of God in Christ Jesus for you. (1 Thessalonians 5:18)

Think Rightly

Finally, brethren, whatever things are true, whatever things are noble, whatever things are just, whatever things are pure, whatever things are lovely, whatever things are of good report, if there is any virtue and if there is anything praiseworthy—meditate on these things. (Philippians 4:8)

Be Pure & Holy

as obedient children, not conforming yourselves to the former lusts, as in your ignorance; but as He who called you is holy, you also be holy in all your conduct, because it is written, "Be holy, for I am holy. (1 Peter 1:14–16)

Bear Fruit for the Lord

that you may walk worthy of the Lord, fully pleasing Him, being fruitful in every good work and increasing in the knowledge of God (Colossians 1:10)

Be a Wise Steward

As each one has received a gift, minister it to one another, as good stewards of the manifold grace of God. (1 Peter 4:10)

Beware of the Devil's Tactics

For all that is in the world—the lust of the flesh, the lust of the eyes, and the pride of life—is not of the Father but is of the world. (1 John 2:16)

Persevere in Trials

Blessed is the man who endures temptation; for when he has been approved, he will receive the crown of life which the Lord has promised to those who love Him. (James 1:12)

Indeed we count them blessed who endure. You have heard of the perseverance of Job and seen the end intended by the Lord—that the Lord is very compassionate and merciful. (James 5:11)

Remember Your Time is Short & Limited

whereas you do not know what will happen tomorrow. For what is your life? It is even a vapor that appears for a little time and then vanishes away. (James 4:14)

Remember Our Future Judgment

For we must all appear before the judgment seat of Christ, that each one may receive the things done in the body, according to what he has done, whether good or bad. (2 Corinthians 5:10)

Hope in Christ

Therefore gird up the loins of your mind, be sober, and rest your hope fully upon the grace that is to

> be brought to you at the revelation of Jesus Christ (1 Peter 1:13)

This is a breathtaking list and is impossible to live out in the flesh alone. If you do not quench the Spirit, but are Spirit-filled, yielding to God and His Word, you will be able to bear fruit unto the Lord.

Remember, it is God who is at work in you, both to will and to do his good pleasure. May you truly take every opportunity to R.E.F.L.E.C.T. the glory of God in prayer.

PRAYER SCHEDULE EXAMPLE

Create a schedule or set a reminder on your phone to take several moments out of your day to pray.

8 AM:

12 PM:

6 PM:

10 PM:

YOUR PRAYER SCHEDULE

CHAPTER SUMMARY

Step 7 – Take Every Opportunity

- **Be Diligent** (2 Peter 1:5-11)
- **Remember Christ's Death, Burial, and Resurrection** (1 Corinthians 15:1-4)
- **Remember God's Forgiveness** (2 Corinthians 5:21, Colossians 2:13-14)
- **Be Thankful** (1 Thessalonians 5:18)
- **Think Rightly** (Philippians 4:8)
- **Be Pure & Holy** (1 John 3:3, 1 Peter 1:14-16)
- **Bear Fruit for the Lord** (Colossians 1:10)
- **Be a Wise Steward** (1 Peter 4:10)
- **Beware of the Devil's Tactics** (1 John 2:16)
- **Persevere in Trials** (James 1:12, James 5:11)
- **Remember Your Time is Short & Limited** (James 4:14)
- **Remember Our Future Judgment** (2 Corinthians 5:10)
- **Hope in Christ** (1 Peter 1:13)

GROUP DISCUSSION

1. List several ways you can encourage one another to pray regularly. How could you pray more?

2. What reminders could you add to the list above?

> Review

Final Word

I will extol You, my God, O King; And I will bless Your name forever and ever. Every day I will bless You, And I will praise Your name forever and ever. Great is the LORD, and greatly to be praised; And His greatness is unsearchable. One generation shall praise Your works to another, And shall declare Your mighty acts. I will meditate on the glorious splendor of Your majesty, And on Your wondrous works. Men shall speak of the might of Your awesome acts, And I will declare Your greatness. They shall utter the memory of Your great goodness, And shall sing of Your righteousness. The LORD is gracious and full of compassion, Slow to anger and great in mercy. The LORD is good to all, And His tender mercies are over all His works. All Your works shall praise You, O LORD, And Your saints shall bless You. They shall speak of the glory of Your kingdom, And talk of Your power, To make known to the sons of men His mighty acts, And the glorious majesty of His kingdom. Your kingdom is an everlasting kingdom, And Your dominion endures throughout all generations. The LORD upholds all who fall, And raises up all who are bowed down. The eyes of all look expectantly to You, And You give them their food in due season.

> You open Your hand And satisfy the desire of every living thing. The LORD is righteous in all His ways, Gracious in all His works. The LORD is near to all who call upon Him, To all who call upon Him in truth. He will fulfill the desire of those who fear Him; He also will hear their cry and save them. The LORD preserves all who love Him, But all the wicked He will destroy. My mouth shall speak the praise of the LORD, And all flesh shall bless His holy name Forever and ever. (Psalm 145)

What an amazing psalm reflecting the glory of God in prayer. I encourage you to read, study, and integrate the psalms into your prayer time for growing and knowing how to pray to the Lord.

As we bring our time of studying prayer to a close, consider the following questions:

- What if Hannah had not prayed for a son and there was no Samuel?
- What if David had not prayed and recorded his psalms?
- What if Stephen had not prayed aloud in front of Saul?
- What if Paul and Silas had not prayed at midnight? Would the Philippian jailer have come to know the Lord?

Fortunately, these faithful believers did pray, and we can read about the glorious ways God answered these prayers. But what about you?

Question: What would your life and the life of those you know be like without prayer? Could there be someone you know who has never been prayed for by another Christian?

As you consider the impact of prayer, you truly are at a fork in the road. To the left is prayerlessness and to the right is prayerfulness. How will you live? May you go forth in the Spirit, continuing, persevering, and unwavering in prayer. May you pray nobly and boldly reflecting the glory of God in prayer!

Let us pray.

Heavenly Father, you are the Almighty, El Shaddai, the Powerful. You are the Creator and Redeemer. Profound and lofty are your ways and thoughts. Mighty are your words and deeds. Do not let me sin in the weakness of my flesh nor forsake your Word of truth that is life and light. I plead Lord, change me. Move me to pray. Bring me to your throne room, sit me down, and teach me your ways. Illuminate my mind to understand your Word of truth so that I might not sin against you. Help me to pray according to your will and Word. Transform my life to be a vessel of honor, rather than dishonor. Help me to reflect your Son, Jesus Christ, to others by the power of your

Holy Spirit. Help me to be alert to the needs of others. Help me to love You and show compassion to people I meet. Let me not despair when others reject me for loving You and following your ways. Help me to be courageous and steadfast when others turn against me, because they hate You and your Truth. Give me the courage to proclaim your Gospel, the good news that our sins may be forgiven through repentance and faith in your Perfect Son. Oh, I long for you to rule and reign on this earth. I look forward to your glorious kingdom. I wait patiently for your return. Help me to persevere and not lose hope.

This I continually pray to you Father, through Your Son Jesus Christ, by the help of Your Holy Spirit.

Amen.

> Appendix 1

Jesus' 7 Principles of Prayer

The Apostle John wrote in John 21:25 "And there are also many other things that Jesus did, which if they were written one by one, I suppose that even the world itself could not contain the books that would be written. Amen."

The Apostle John understood the limitations of books and as I studied the prayers of Jesus, it became clear that the following seven principles are by no means an exhaustive list. However, may you find them encouraging, challenging, and a wonderful guide to help you excel still more in reflecting the glory of God in prayer.

Seven Key Principles of Prayer

Principle #1 – Any Time is a Good Time to Pray
Jesus did not use formulas or repetitious prayers when praying. He prayed often and at various times, conversing with His Father in a straightforward manner.

A. **Pray Often** (Luke 5:16, Mark 1:35)
The underlying Greek tenses of the verbs in these Biblical texts emphasize prayer was a customary and habitual practice of Jesus.

B. **Pray at Different Times** (Mark 1:35, Matthew 14:23, Luke 6:12)
Because Jesus prayed often, we find Him praying: before dawn, during daylight, after sunset, and sometimes all night. Regardless of the circumstances Jesus always prayed in the Spirit, being alert with all perseverance and petition (Ephesians 6:18).

Principle #2 – Any Place is a Good Place to Pray

The second principle of prayer is that neither people nor your location should interfere with prayer. Throughout Jesus' ministry, He found a place to pray despite the constant demands of the people. On some occasions, this required Jesus to withdraw completely from people. On other occasions, He withdrew with several or more disciples. There are even times when He remained with others and prayed in their presence. There are times when Jesus was alone, but the Scriptures do not always mention Him praying. However, because of Jesus' pattern of prayer, we can deduce He was praying in His solitude.

A. **Find Solitude**
There are several examples where Jesus withdrew to be alone and pray. For example, the temptation

in the wilderness (Luke 4:1, Matt 4:1, Mark 1:12). We can assume that Jesus prayed throughout this temptation, although the Scriptures do not explicitly mention prayer. A second example would be when Christ withdrew from Galilee after the news that John the Baptist had been killed (Matthew 14:1–14, Mark 6:14–52). Prior to His betrayal by Judas, Jesus withdrew to Mount Olivet most likely to pray alone (Luke 21:34–38). Regardless of circumstances and what was yet to take place, Jesus made it a priority to be alone in prayer with God the Father.

B. **Prayer with Friends**

We see Jesus bringing along several companions for prayer. One example is at the Mount of Transfiguration mentioned in Luke 9:28–36. Another example would be the high priestly prayer of Jesus in the upper room in John 17:1-26. Once Jesus rebuked His disciples for interfering with His desire to lay hands on the children for prayer (Matthew 19:13-15).

C. **Pray in Public Places**

The Lord Jesus Christ would pray before a large crowd and publicly address God the Father. This was to demonstrate the unique relationship between Himself and God, His Father. For example, in Matthew 11:20–30, Jesus praises His Father in prayer before the multitudes for those who believed despite the unrepentant cities of

Chorazin, Capernaum, and Bethsaida. In John 11:1–44, before raising Lazarus from the dead, Jesus thanks God with a public prayer.

Principle #3 – Pray for All Decisions and Events

Jesus validates the need to seek guidance in prayer in anticipation of upcoming decisions and events. Seeking God's wisdom (James 1:5-8) must never be neglected regardless of how big or small the decision or event.

A. **Pray Before Significant Decisions**

One of the more remarkable passages is Luke 6:12-16 in which Jesus prays through the decision to choose the twelve apostles. We can conclude that Jesus communed with the Father in a specific prayer about a single decision, even setting aside the priority of sleep.

B. **Pray Before Significant Events**

In one of the most revealing passages into the mind and heart of Christ regarding His death on the cross, we see three prayers by the Lord Jesus Christ at Gethsemane (Matthew 26:36-46, Mark 14:32–42; Luke 22:39–46). Here we have Jesus withdrawing first with several close disciples, and then withdrawing from them to pray alone. We see how Jesus prayed concerning His death on the cross for man's sin. In agony, Jesus prayed fervently. Jesus models for us how to pray in the most difficult of circumstances.

Principle #4 – Pray Throughout the Ministry

In the trench-work of ministry, where people demand attention, you must not neglect prayer. No person or circumstance should take precedence over prayer. Whether Jesus is being baptized, discussing the death of a loved one, or even being interrupted by inquiring individuals, He prays. His ministry is characterized by prayer.

A. **Jesus Prays at the Beginning of Ministry**

   In Luke 3:21-22 we see Jesus praying, heaven opens, and the Holy Spirit descends upon Him in bodily form like a dove. Between the baptism of Jesus and the temptation in the wilderness by Satan, we see Jesus inaugurating His ministry with prayer.

B. **Jesus Prays During Difficult Times**

   In John 11, we read about the death and resurrection of Lazarus. The words Jesus prayed for Lazarus to rise from the dead are not in the Scriptures. However, we do read in John 11:41-42 that Jesus gave thanks to God the Father in the presence of the crowd for hearing His prayer before raising Lazarus. As the people were mourning Lazarus' death, Jesus was grieving; yet, He prays. Learn from Jesus. He was continually in prayer no matter how busy or distressed.

C. Jesus Prays at Busy Times

The Passover before Jesus' crucifixion was fast approaching, and He was answering questions from the Greeks in John 12:20-50. As Jesus taught the people that He must die, He petitioned God the Father to glorify the Father's name. Soon after this prayer, the voice of God His Father speaks forth from heaven for all to hear (John 12:28). It is important to note that although Jesus is busy ministering to the people and Jesus Himself is grieving, Jesus prays not for Himself but for God's glory.

Principle #5 - Prayer is the Concluding Activity

At the close of ministering to others, you must pray. You need to reflect on the blessings, successes, and failures, and then come to God the Father with adoration, confession, and thanksgiving. Do not be tempted to neglect prayer.

A. Jesus Prayed After Feeding the 5000

It is amazing to see that even after a significant event or miracle, Jesus allocates time to pray. He sends the disciples away in a boat and heads alone to the mountains to pray (Matthew 14:23, Mark 6:46, John 6:15). Although exhausted from ministering to others, Jesus always found time to pray when the activities were over.

B. Jesus Prayed After the 70 Returned

In the passage of Luke 10:21-22 the seventy disciples that Jesus had sent out earlier (Luke 10:1) have returned rejoicing. Christ expresses divine joy in a public prayer of praise to God the Father. Christ manifests to us the priority of prayer after ministering to others.

Principle #6 – Pray for Your Enemies

The Lord Jesus Christ portrays the principle of prayer in suffering and persecution like no other individual in the Bible or in all of history. We see that under the severest of trials, at the height of His persecution and pain on the cross, prayer permeates His substitutional, sacrificial suffering for sin. On the cross, the Scriptures reveal to us seven sayings of Jesus; three of which are specific prayers.

A. Commencement of the Crucifixion

Jesus utters the following words, recorded in Luke 23:34, as the first saying on the cross, "Father, forgive them; for they do not know what they are doing." This is an intercessory prayer to God the Father on behalf of His tormentors. Jesus' perfect example, in spite of intense pain, shows us how to pray at the inauguration of our trials. Jesus Christ, despite the injurious nature of the cross, looks past His immediate and painful circumstances and commits to prayer the needs of His ignorant enemies.

B. Continuance of the Crucifixion

The fourth saying of Jesus on the cross is found in Matthew 27:46, "Eli, Eli, lama sabachthani?" that is, "My God, My God, why have You forsaken Me?" This prayer, in the form of a question, looks back to Psalm 22. These solemn words reveal Jesus' anguish at being separated from God the Father for the first and only time, because of His sin-bearing (Isaiah 52:14-53:12). The fact that Jesus turned to prayer while suffering for sins He did not commit, should compel us to pray during intense moments of suffering.

C. Conclusion of the Crucifixion

In Luke 23:46 we read, "Father, into your hands I commit my spirit." The seventh and final saying of Jesus looks back to Psalm 31:5, consummating with prayer the completion of His cross-work to atone for your sin. This prayer is a reminder that when the end is near, pray!

Principle #7 – Pray for One Another

The principle of intercessory prayer is modeled by Jesus. Although most of the intercessory prayers by Jesus are not recorded, the Scriptures do reveal that Jesus had interceded regularly for people.

A. Prayer for Peter

In Luke 22:32 we discover that Satan had requested to sift Peter like wheat. However, we read that Jesus had prayed for Peter at some point earlier. Although we do not know when He prayed, it reveals that Jesus never lost sight of others and their needs, amid the demands and pressures of life and ministry.

B. Priestly Prayer

In John 17:1-26, which takes place in the upper room before Jesus' betrayal, we have the longest single prayer of Jesus found in the New Testament. The Lord Jesus is with the apostles. Jesus had washed their feet (John 13:1-20), the Passover meal had concluded, the Lord's Supper was instituted (Matthew 26:26-29), Judas had left to betray Jesus (John 13:21-30), and right before they sang a hymn and departed, Jesus took time to pray. Not only did Jesus pray for the soul-saving work He was to carry out on the cross, but He also prayed for the disciples and future believers. These petitions were not about wealth, prestige, or worldly influence; but that present and future believers would be kept from evil and the Evil One, be holy in a sinful world, be eligible for service, and be delivered safely to their heavenly home.

What can we conclude?

Life has its ebbs and flows, but prayerful communion with the Father must be a constant for every born-again believer. To truly prioritize prayer in a busy schedule one must pray before, during, and after any and all activities. It should not matter if you are in a season of peace, prosperity, painful trials, or even persecution. Never cease from petitioning on behalf of others and for yourself.

Jesus exemplified this pattern throughout His ministry, whether He was alone, before few, or before many. Even though we have few examples of the words Jesus prayed, His prayer life reveals prayer was His priority.

His example is sufficient to compel us to examine the priority of prayer in our life. Let us not forget, Christ was sinless; He had the perfect relationship with the Father, and yet, He made prayer a priority. Oh, that you and I would bow the knee before God our Maker and do the same.

> Appendix 2

The Lord's / Disciples' Prayer

The Lord's Prayer, also named the Disciples' Prayer, is not a prayer to be vainly repeated (Matthew 6:5-9) but is a template for praying. Below is a guide to help you pray through this amazing prayer.

Matthew 6:9-15

LOVING GOD

Our Father in heaven

- ACKNOWLEDGE that prayer begins solely with God the Father who is in heaven

Hallowed be your name.

- APPROACH God with reverence and respect

Your kingdom come.

- AFFIRM God's reign over all things

Your will be done on earth, as it is in heaven.

- ADVOCATE God's will to be accomplished

LOVING PEOPLE

Give us this day our daily bread.

- ASK God to supply your essential needs

And forgive us our debts, as we forgive our debtors.

- APPEAL for forgiveness and reconciliation

And do not lead us into temptation,

- ADORE the paths of righteousness and truth

but deliver us from the evil one.

- ACT wisely to avoid bondage to sin and the Devil

For Yours is the kingdom and the power and the glory, forever. Amen.

- AMEN the glorious eternal rule and reign of God

> Appendix 3

THE NAMES OF GOD

There are various names for God in the Old Testament. Many of these names reflect the character, attributes, and actions of God. I have listed several below with the name of God and one passage for reading, meditating, and praying.

NOTE: In the 16th century, a translator in Germany took the vowels of Adonai and combined them with the consonants for YHVH to create Jehovah (*YaHoVah).* Today, scholars use Yahweh for God's name.

Yahweh - I Am
(Exodus 3:10-22)

Adonai - The Lord
(Psalm 54)

Elohim - God the Creator
(Genesis 1:1-2:3)

El Elyon - God Most High
(Genesis 14:17–24)

El Elohe Israel - The God of Israel
(Genesis 33:18–20)

El Shaddai - God Almighty
(Genesis 17:1–22)

Yahweh Rophe'ekha – The Lord is your Healer
(Exodus 15:22–27)

Yahweh Ro'i - The Lord is my Shepherd
(Psalm 23)

Yahweh Shammah - The Lord is There
(Ezekiel 48:30–35)

Yahweh Tseva'oth (Sabaoth) - The Lord of Hosts
(Isaiah 2:12–22)

Yahweh Tsidqenu - The Lord our Righteousness
(Jeremiah 23:1-8)

Yahweh Meqaddishkhem - The Lord who Sanctifies
(Exodus 31:12–18)

Yahweh Yir'eh - The Lord will Provide
(Genesis 22:1-19)

> Appendix 4

12 Categories of Prayer

Focus is critical for any activity and prayer is no different. One way to stay focused is to create a list of groups for whom you will pray for regularly. A list, such as the one below, can help you to pray for a wider range of people beyond your close family members and friends. Feel free to customize this list for your personal preferences.

01-Immediate family
02-Extended family
03-Your local church leadership and members
04-Ministries and activities of the local church
05-Missionaries
06-Co-workers and colleagues
07-Friends, neighbors, and acquaintances
08-Government leaders currently in authority
09-Local community
10-Countries
11-Recent events
12-Personal needs

> Appendix 5

Prayer Journals

If you are wondering how to journal your prayers and what is the best strategy, let me offer the following suggestions.

First, keep it simple. Acquire a notebook or use your phone and organize your prayer journal as follows:

Date and Time
Person Needing Prayer
Prayer Request Details
Date and Time of Answered Prayer
Answered Prayer Details
Date to Follow Up

Second, review and update the journal at the end of each week. This makes the maintenance of the prayer journal manageable. If the prayer receives an answer, note the date and how the prayer was answered. I recommend putting a 'yes' or 'no' next to your answered prayer and note unique information when the prayer is answered.

Third, once a month, review all unanswered prayers and then reach out to individuals whose prayers remained unanswered. You will be an encouragement to others by seeking a prayer update from them.

Fourth, do not be afraid to ask God for something significant, but be sure it is according to His Word and not for selfish gain.

Fifth, if there are individuals in your life that you are praying for on a regular basis (parents, siblings, children, grandchildren, a close friend, etc.), consider journaling in a separate notebook devoted to them exclusively. At some point in the future, give them your prayer journal so they can see how God has answered prayer. This can be a great spiritual encouragement.

> Appendix 6

Prayer Discipleship

Start a small group that meets once a week or twice a month and pray together for one hour. We have a couple in our church that has been taking part in one of these small prayer meetings for over four years. They recommend having some structure in the prayer time and suggest using the following topics as a guide for prayer: praising God, confessing sin, praying for leaders, reading the Scriptures, interceding on behalf of others (such as for the local church and church leaders, Christian businesses, families, and those in authority), giving thanks, singing hymns, recalling and affirming God's promises.

Consider meeting in different locations or even conducting a prayer-walk through a neighborhood. However, be respectful should somone ask you to leave. But before you leave, ask them if you could pray for them. Who knows, the Lord may use this encounter to save their soul.

Make sure your group is not too large, ten or less is ideal. Be prepared to share the Gospel and bring along some Gospel tracts with your local church's contact information.

> Appendix 7

A Prayer Class

If this book has been a blessing to you, consider leading a small group teaching and applying these praying principles. Imagine the possibilities of multiple prayer groups meeting around the world focused on praying more effectively. Who knows the kind of impact this could have for God's kingdom!

Curriculum

We have developed a curriculum for learning prayer principles so you can R.E.F.L.E.C.T. the glory of God in prayer.

Learn More

http://www.ReflectTheGloryOfGodInPrayer.com
http://www.LearnLogos.com/pray

Email

If you have questions, please email me at
pray@learnlogos.com

> Appendix 8

The Intercessors

Charles Spurgeon, the 19th century preacher, pastored at the Metropolitan Tabernacle Church in London. He understood firsthand the role of intercessors and the power of prayer.

When people from all over the world would visit the church to learn the secret of his success, he would take these individuals on a tour to a room in the basement. There he would reveal a chamber full of people praying on their knees, interceding on behalf of others before God. Charles Spurgeon affectionately referred to this space as the "powerhouse of the church." He would go on to say, "If the engine room is out of action, then the whole mill will grind to a halt. We cannot expect blessing if we do not ask."

At Brookside Baptist Church, we have nearly one hundred godly ladies devoted to prayer as our "powerful engine of prayer." We are so blessed and indebted to their sacrificial love to God and us. May you cultivate in your church a ministry of intercessors.

> Appendix 9

People Needing Prayer

Please use the following space to write down the names of individuals needing prayer.

ABOUT THE AUTHOR

In 1995, author John David Fallahee was delivered from bondage to alcohol and drugs by his Lord and Savior Jesus Christ.

Through prayer, Scripture reading, and discipleship in the local church, John found redemption, power, and hope.

This book shares seven praying principles he has learned from studying the Word of God and walking in the fear of the Lord and in the comfort of the Holy Spirit.

John is currently serving as the discipleship pastor at Brookside Baptist Church in Brookfield, Wisconsin.

Made in the USA
Monee, IL
02 July 2023

38290763R00090